As *Eat, Pray, Love* i
raucous, independent, and contented life.

– William M. Akers, Author, *Your Screenplay Sucks!*, *Mrs. Ravenbach's Way*

Kelley Baker distills his own brand of travel liquor and bottles it up for you in this book.

– Don Campbell, Writer, Musician, Road Dog

A wonderful piece of modern-day Americana.

– Fiona Young-Brown, Author:
A Culinary History of Kentucky: Burgoo, Beer Cheese, & Goetta

What a trip! I was there (in parts), and I much prefer Kelley's memory to my own. I love this book!

– Daniel Boyd, Author/Filmmaker, *Chillers, Carbon, Salt*

Old dogs and the open road. A match made in heaven.

– Jeff Pollard, *POLLARDdesign*

A great read that will make you laugh a lot, cry a little and appreciate the important people (two legged or four) in your life more.

– Nic Brown, Author:
Werewolves, Zombies & Leprechauns: Tales From the World of Werewolf For Hire

THE
ANGRY FILMMAKER
PRESENTS

ANOTHER
KELLEY BAKER
JAG

ROAD DOG

Kelley Baker

ANGRY FILMMAKER

© 2016 Kelley Baker / All rights reserved.

No part of this publication may be reproduced, stored in a retrieval system, or transmitted in any form or by any means, electronic, mechanical, photocopying, recording, or otherwise without the written permission of the author.

To order additional copies, please contact us —
Sales@AngryFilmmaker.com or visit our website at
AngryFilmmaker.com

ISBN-13: 978-1540713520
ISBN-10: 1540713520

This book is a work of non-fiction—for the most part anyway, but just in case you think you recognize someone...

People, places, and events are fictional and any resemblance to actual persons living or dead is purely coincidental.

Printed in the United States of America.

AngryFilmmaker.com

For Moses—
The best damn traveling companion
I could ever have.

For Harris Mattarazzo—
Who keeps me out of jail
and is a good friend, even when I'm not.

For Kid—
"Just remember,
it's not all late-night diners and pancakes."

ACKNOWLEDGMENTS

I want to thank Don Campbell for his tireless editing of this book. Jeff Pollard for his amazing design work, feedback and friendship. Margie Yap for her constant advice and pushing me to follow my dreams. Fiona Baker for being my inspiration. Kim Blair for her unwavering support above and beyond. Jon Gann for putting up with me and putting me up. William Akers for his incisive feedback and a place to write. Brian Johnson for his great ideas. Joe Heyen for always having room for us. Danny Boyd for his insight and beers. Michelle Mower for her friendship. And Chris Hansen for not asking me not to swear.

I want to thank the following people without their help the tours and this book would have never gotten off the ground. Debby Dietrich, Harris Mattarazzo, Cari Callis, Bill & Shawn Dever, Robert Tinnell, Nic Brown & Fiona Young-Brown, Nathan Wagoner, Rob Kates, Nemo Chu, Jim Carrier & Trish O'Kane, Amber & Jeff Whitlach, William Bittner, Jim LeBrecht, Tim & Leilani McHugh, Dana Driskel, Glenn Campbell, Arati Moses, Alan & Miss Courtney, Mark Nobles, David Merrill, Jim Fields, IFC Kansas City, Joe & Cyndi Gaudin, Sally & Mark Orloff, Paul Sabal, Lorah Sheltmire Steiner, Prema Thiagarajah, NFI, Paul Lewis, Rick Vaicius, David Nicholas & Melanie Maxcey Nicholas, Sam Connelly, Chris Huntley, Andy Garrison,

Aric Hornig, Freddi Tachman Carlip, Rob Sabal, Angel Vasquez, John Otterbacher, Jay Horan, Joe Scherrman, Suzie Wright, Diana Vaicius, Marc Rose, Matt Meyer, and Vince Columbo.

I would be remiss in not thanking Jim & Mary Baker, Martin Vavra, Galaxy Sailor Productions, Stephen Dixon, and Josh & Joanna Cross. If I have missed anyone I apologize. This was one long group effort and I'm sorry if you fell through the cracks.

And to all of the bartenders, baristas, cashiers, fast food servers, chefs, cooks, and anyone else who touched my food or drink on these tours, a heartfelt thank you for not poisoning me or Moses.

"When the legend becomes fact, print the legend."

– From *The Man Who Shot Liberty Valance*

"Truth is stranger than fiction, but it is because Fiction is obliged to stick to possibilities; Truth isn't."

– Mark Twain

"I can say with 100% accuracy that this book is mostly true."

– Kelley Baker

Of course I've changed some names, moved a few things around and even combined some stuff. And sure I've probably embellished a few things here and there, but overall it's fairly accurate. At least as accurate as my memory would lead me to believe. How much you want to believe is entirely up to you.

FATHER/DAUGHTER SUMMER TOUR
POST #7

My daughter Fiona was fifteen when she wrote this out on tour with me.

General Tips for being on the road with the one and only Angry Filmmaker:
1. No car ride is long to my dad. You mention that an eight-hour drive is a long one? He'll smirk and tell you of all the times he drove twenty-hours straight to get to a teaching gig in time.
2. Learn how to entertain yourself with road signs. They're easy to make fun of and incredibly hilarious if you do it right.
3. Don't get weirded out about sleeping in a different place almost every night. Seriously, it's not a big deal.
4. Be polite to all of his students, even if they all ask you the same questions and tend to be obnoxious and think they know more about film than anyone else. You will never see them again. You can deal with "What grade are you in?" and "So do you want to be a filmmaker too?" for 15 minutes. After that, you have every right to go hide in the back.
5. Get used to the smell of dog. Moses is always a good companion, but he can get a little stinky after what feels like a billion hours in the van.

6. Be a trooper. It's not always fun (okay so it is 95 percent of the time), but be helpful. It's an easy thing.
7. Don't be a tourist. It's just not cool. Hang with the locals. Act like a local.
8. Don't pack a lot. There are a lot of opportunities to do laundry if you stay with the right people. Plus its fewer bags you have to pack. Much easier when you end up leaving places at 6 a.m.
9. Sleep in the car. It makes time go by faster.
10. Enjoy the experience. You do not live the life of my dad. Touring is not business as usual.

INTRODUCTION

It's two a.m. My eyes hurt. My head is pounding and I can't get any radio stations. Not that it matters.

My econo-box rental car is rocketing down a dark two-lane road somewhere in the Texas hill country. I'm driving a Suzuki Esteem. It should be called a Low-Esteem. This thing is pathetic.

I left the Desert Rose Film Festival a few hours ago trying to make a six a.m. flight out of Austin.

The festival was good, my film *Kicking Bird* went over well, and I sold some merch. A producer from New York who had a two-million-dollar film there watched *Kicking Bird* and couldn't believe I made it for less than $10,000. "If you ever get a budget you're gonna be dangerous!"

A good couple days in the life of a touring filmmaker.

I should've stayed the night. The after party was just getting out of hand when I left. God only knows what's happening now.

I stop for gas and coffee at a tiny store/gas station in the middle of nowhere. The wrinkled old crow behind the counter is straight out of a Wes Craven film.

"Where ya headed?"

"Austin."

"That's three more hours. Seen any deer yet?"

"Nope, just the road."

"Mild winter. Never seen it this bad. They reproduce like rabbits. Ya see the skid marks? People trying to avoid 'em..."

So what is this, Night of the Living Bambi, I think to myself.

"Been a lot a wrecks. People dyin'..."

"I'll be careful."

"They jump right out in front of ya. No time to stop. That car of yours don't look too solid."

No shit, I think to myself.

"Ya shoulda got a bigger car. Like a truck or somethin... Sometimes even that don't help."

"How much for the coffee?"

"Ya ever seen a car after it's hit a deer?"

I shake my head.

"Ya wonder how anybody survived."

"The coffee?"

"On the house."

"Thanks! You have a good night."

"Ya never see 'em till 'it too late. Be careful."

I leave thinking just another bat-shit crazy person working nights for too long...

Back on the road I notice the skid marks. They're all heading off the road.

Are those eyes staring at me from the shoulder?

Is that a deer? I zoom past.

Another?

I'm convinced I'm seeing lots of bright eyes staring at me just out of range of my headlights. If those are deer I don't want to assist them in their suicide plans.

The Low-Esteem whines as I hurdle blindly through the pitch-black Texas night. I feel like I'm driving a goddamn go-kart.

There are no freeways between Odessa and Austin. I have no GPS, just some notes scribbled on a napkin David gave me before I left. He said this was the fastest way. The fastest way to hell probably.

I hit scan and the radio finally finds something. Mariachi music. I hit scan again and it goes all the way through the band and comes back to the mariachis.

I let it play.

I shiver. The air conditioning is cranked up to keep me awake. I'm freezing. But it works.

All these eyes staring at me is fucking creepy. Not even sure they're really there. My hands are sweating. They hurt. Econo-box car seats never get comfortable.

Why didn't I upgrade to something like a Taurus? Oh yeah, I'm Scottish.

I hit the scan button again, there's got to be something besides mariachis. The tuner stops. I hear a familiar tune buried in the static. I let it play.

The night gets darker, my eyes hurt. Even with the air conditioning blasting I start to sweat. I check the clock. It's two-thirty. Miles to go.

I'm feeling a presence, something strange. I'm exhausted and I can't put my finger on this weird feeling. Something is bothering me.

I'm so goddamn tired I just want to get to the airport without dying. How much fucking longer…

I see things that I know are not there. More and more eyes stare back at me. This is fucked up!

I suddenly realize the familiar song on the radio is Pink Floyd's *Lunatic*. I shut it off when the dude starts laughing.

I'm not scared. I just need to concentrate. There's nothing out there. I'm not scared!

Did Kerouac or Steinbeck ever have nights like this?

I should've stayed and left in the morning. I coulda gotten an afternoon flight. I could be partying right now…

I've still got two hours to go.

My mind wanders as I look out beyond the headlights.

I remember that old joke.

What's the last thing that goes through a bugs mind as it hits the windshield?

Its asshole!

PILOT is MY CO-DOG

Our story starts in the Garden of Eden. Not that one. The one in Lucas, Kansas.

S. P. Dinsmoor's Garden of Eden.

The wind blows ferociously across the Kansas prairie, because it's…Kansas.

I'm standing next to a too-skinny woman dressed in black who reminds me of a meth addict. With teeth. Dinsmoor's lying in front of us. He's seen better days.

S.P. Dinsmoor is a mummy.

The woman next to me is probably not a meth addict, but Dinsmoor is definitely a mummy.

He looks creepy as hell. I'm happy it's the middle of the day and not late at night.

The heavy metal door on the mausoleum slams shut. I can't

speak for the others but I certainly jumped.

I don't know who did the work on him, but I'm sure he didn't pay full price. His hair's still kind of there, as are his teeth. He isn't a skull yet, but there isn't a lot of flesh left on his face. A lot of things have sunk in. His eyes are there, sort of. He's wearing a nice suit, at least it was at one time. It seems to be mildewing. I don't think the glass case, coffin, tomb or whatever the hell he's in, is airtight. The suit is definitely throwing me off, but what the hell was I expecting, he'd be wrapped in bandages?

Seeing any guy who's been mummified outside of the British Museum is pretty weird. I'm wondering if he's cursed?

S.P. Dinsmoor is considered a "folk artist." Jon found out about him on his phone as we were speeding through Kansas. He wanted to stop somewhere and our choices were this or the "World's Largest Ball of Twine" in Cawker City. We opted for the mummy.

There are concrete statues all over the yard; most are mounted high on wooden frames. These statues are all handmade and pretty crude. Hence the phrase "folk artist," I suppose.

It appears Dinsmoor had a problem with authority figures. His statues are mostly of men: the evil banker, the evil minister, and the evil politician. I think there's a trend here.

I wonder what Moses would have thought of all of this?

Let me back up a bit…

It's weird to be on tour with a dog that *isn't* Moses. I'm with my buddy Jon and his dog Pilot. Pilot's a great dog but his personality is different, his energy is different. It's also weird sharing space in the van with someone else.

Jon's a filmmaker and the founder of the DC Shorts Film Festival. Every year I go to the film festival, speak, do workshops, go to parties, hang out, drink, and generally have a great time. The DC Shorts Film Festival is usually the kick-off of my fall tour.

Jon's bothered me a lot over the years about going out on tour, so we're doing it. Actually it's only half a tour. I've already been on the road four weeks when Jon joins me. Of course Pilot comes with us.

Jon loves to have adventures. Don't we all? But Jon's different. When he says he wants to see or do something he just does it, while most of us are making up excuses as to why we can't.

When I first started touring it was all about adventure. Like taking three days off and driving to the Outer Banks of North Carolina to see Kitty Hawk, walk along the Atlantic, check out the Cape Hatteras Lighthouse, and learn about pirates. Plus, Moses had never gone swimming in the Atlantic and I knew that was a dream of his, although we never discussed it.

Somewhere on all of our tours I lost my sense of adventure. I was booking as many stops as possible to make money. As long as I was on the road I needed to make the best use of my time and apparently that meant no adventures. I was always rushing to get to the next gig. Had I seen everything I wanted to? Or did I just get tired? When you're in the middle of touring you don't know.

You just wake up one day and realize that you've been traveling for a long time and not seeing anything. That's when you have to shake things up.

Jon, like Ray Bradbury, still looks at things like a thirteen-year-old boy. He has this enthusiasm when it comes to travel and new experiences.

One time in Seattle he got us tickets to the Boeing factory tour. Why the hell would I want to tour the Boeing factory?

"To see where they make the jets we spend so much time in," Jon said.

It wasn't something I'd thought much about and, even though I live just down the road from Seattle, I never knew you could tour Boeing. And that's what I love about Jon. He makes me look at things differently. I need this. And by the way, the tour was really interesting.

Meanwhile, back at The Garden Of Eden...

S.P. Dinsmoor's house is something of a "museum," where for a mere six dollars you can wander around and check out his barbwire collection. It's all neatly arranged in the basement on boards that hang on the wall. And it's huge. Who knew there were that many types of barbed wire?

For fifteen dollars you could have the guided tour from the too-skinny woman. We opted for the self-tour. Wandering around the house was nothing special. I'm not sure what I expected. It was just a house with some old furniture in it. The real attraction was Dinsmoor himself and his mausoleum.

According to Jon's iPhone, S.P. built the mausoleum out back where he and his wife now reside. She's encased in concrete and he's resting under a piece of clear glass.

The mausoleum is in the backyard but to our dismay, the door is locked. The wind has picked up and, being in Kansas, I'm thinking about tornadoes, wicked witches, scarecrows, and a small dog. We spot Too Skinny coming back from God-knows-where in a hurry.

I ask her about the mausoleum and without breaking stride she assures me she'll be right back to open it.

Sure enough a few minutes later she's back with a key. She apologizes saying she had to deal with one of her grandchildren over at school. Jon, ever the gentleman, comments that she looks too young to be a grandmother.

She smiles as she opens the door. "You're very kind, but I'm almost forty."

We walk in and there's S.P laid out in front of us.

After a few minutes of staring at the mummified remains thinking, "What the hell?" I have to ask. "So why's the Mrs. encased in concrete and he's laid out for all the world to see?"

It seems S.P. built his mausoleum a few years before his wife passed and after her death he wanted to mummify her and place her in it. But the town said no, as they often do in a situation like this. I guess it's okay to bury a dog, cat or other pet in the backyard, but burying family members is frowned upon.

So the Mrs. was buried in the town cemetery. Later that night

Dinsmoor returns, digs her up and brings her back home. He places her in the mausoleum, and covers her in a thousand pounds of concrete that he has lying around for his sculptures. That way the city can't come out, dig her up, and return her to the cemetery. He wasn't fucking around.

By the time he died, the town appears to have changed its tune about backyard burials and he's laid to rest under glass on top of her. There's a joke here somewhere and I'll let you come up with your own.

I take a few photos of the body but they don't come out well. And no, there are no shadows or translucent figures in any of my photos but this experience has appeared in a dream or two of mine.

By this time Jon and I are sufficiently creeped out and call it a day. We thank our lovely host and head back to the highway.

This is an important tour for me. It's the first one without Moses and for the first four weeks it feels pretty strange. Moses and I traveled around the U.S. a dozen times together. I'm still looking behind the passenger seat expecting to see him there.

Touring with Jon and Pilot is a huge step for me. It isn't the same, and it'll never be the same, but I need to take that first step.

WHY the FUCK DO I DO THIS?

I was in high school when I first read John Steinbeck's *Travels With Charley*. I thought wouldn't it be great to travel across the country in a camper with your dog?

I followed that with Kerouac's *On The Road*, then *Zen and the Art of Motorcycle Maintenance* (which I couldn't get through – I found it really boring. Obviously I'm not very spiritual). Over the years there were countless other books. I saw *Two Lane Blacktop*, *Easy Rider*, and tons of other road movies.

I had this romantic vision of the US. Okay, not from *Easy Rider* but you get what I mean.

It wasn't until I was in my forties that I finally did it. Fifteen times, give or take. And most of those trips were with my dog, Moses.

Why'd I do it? Did I have some noble quest like Steinbeck

trying to get back in touch with America?

Not really.

I'm an independent filmmaker and I hit the road to show my films. I've made eight short films, some documentaries, and three full-length features. My films were all rejected by distributors, but I felt they deserved an audience. I believed once people saw my films they'd like them.

By the time I started touring I didn't even want a distributor. What I wanted was to reach out to an audience, hopefully my audience. If it worked, great. If not, what the hell? This was my own Don Quixote quest.

Things have changed a lot in the film world since I started making my own films. I studied film at USC, and their focus was on studio films. The films I wanted to make didn't fit in with what the studios wanted.

There was an independent film movement in the early 1980s that I was a part of, and it influenced me.

In the late seventies and early eighties there was a small group of filmmakers that were making films on tiny budgets and getting them into festivals. Not the big film festivals like Cannes and Venice, but smaller festivals that were popping up and they were interested in independent and personal films.

Throughout the eighties and nineties I made short films and documentaries. My films played in a lot of film festivals and some were shown on television. Not just PBS but on Canadian and Australian television as well.

I have what we jokingly refer to as Indie Street Cred, having been the sound designer on six of Gus Van Sant's feature films in addition to making my own.

When I made my first feature *Birddog* I was sure I'd get a distribution deal from someone and I'd be on my way.

Birddog did well on the festival circuit and I screened it for a lot of different distributors.

No one was interested.

None of their reasons had anything to do with story, acting or film quality. All of those things were praised. The common comment was, "We really like your film but we don't know how to market it. What it really needs is a star."

A star? Wait a minute, I thought these people were looking for independent films. Films that were different, challenging. Films that reflected the people who made them. Films that were different than what was coming out of Hollywood. There were independent theaters that were looking for different stuff.

This star crap sounds like something the Hollywood distributors would say. It was then that I realized that the independent film movement was crap! So many of the people who identified themselves as independent were just like the people we were supposed to be an alternative to.

I spent over a year taking *Birddog* to festivals and markets and doing my own distribution screenings. Nothing.

Heavily in debt I said, "Fuck it!" and made another feature.

The Gas Café was darker and more difficult than *Birddog*.

Now I had two films that no distributor wanted, so I made a third, *Kicking Bird*. More accessible, but still dark. And no big name actors, just good performances!

Now what?

IT'S DIY TIME!

I ripped a page out of the punk-rock handbook and put together a tour to show my films around the country. I booked as many places as I could over a two-month period and headed out in a borrowed pick-up truck with a thousand DVDs I had burned on my home computer, one at a time.

I made money so I decided to do it again. This time I bought a second-hand van so Moses could come with me.

In the beginning we were touring twice a year for six-to-eight weeks at a time. I did a fall tour starting after Labor Day and ending in mid-November. The spring tour would go from mid-March to early May.

When my daughter Fiona was eighteen she and I figured out that I'd only spent one entire year at home while she was growing up. She thought that me being on the road was a normal thing and it was weird that her friend's parents came home every night. It made her appreciate the time I was home. It also gave her a love of travel. She went on tour with me at fifteen and loved it!

ODYSSEUS WAS HOMESICK?

People have this romantic notion of being on the road and for the most part it's fun. For a while. It can also be a grind. Waking up every morning in different places wondering what the weather is going to be like. Driving a couple hundred miles a day just to show your film, answer a few questions, find a place to crash, and get up and do it again the next day.

Do I ever get home sick? Of course.

I try not to think about home while I'm on the road. It only makes it worse. I do think about my daughter and we talk at least every other day, if not every day.

I don't start thinking about home until the final week. I allow myself that. If I start thinking about home before then it makes the time go slower and I can get depressed, which I can't afford. You have to put on a road mindset.

When I pull out of Portland on the first morning heading east on Interstate 84 it's an amazing feeling. I'm free. Moses and I are starting a two-month adventure and all of the bullshit of every day life is left behind.

The bullshit isn't really left behind but I'll deal with it in a different way for the next two months.

I love being on the road as the sun comes up. Those early morning hours are glorious. Quiet, very little traffic and watching the sunrise is a perfect way to start a day. The down side is I have difficulty going to bed before midnight. On the road I operate on five to six hours of sleep regularly.

On the fall tour I head straight east into the sunrise as I follow the Columbia River. The scenery in the Columbia Gorge is beautiful, often breath-taking. The sun glistens off one of the most amazing rivers anywhere. And yes, I've crossed the Mississippi dozens of times, but since it flows north-south the sunlight hits it in a totally different way.

The Columbia flows aggressively to the west. On a cold morning I see the white caps on the water and the tall rocky cliffs of the gorge emphasize its beauty and its ruggedness. There are hawks and eagles soaring over the river and every now and again if you're lucky you get to see one dive. There are tugboats and barges working. On the Washington side, long freight trains make their way along the river. At the town of Hood River I watch wind surfers catch air in the early morning light.

To me all of this says new beginnings, new destinations, and new possibilities.

Outside the windshield is the future. I'll be meeting new people, speaking at new venues, catching up with old friends, sharing great meals, and at some point drinking too much and laughing my ass off.

The lure of the road pulls on me when I'm home. A circus clown I know used to say that when he was home for even a few weeks he started to feel like moss was growing on his side and he'd start booking his next trip. I understand that.

BEWARE OF AIR-COOLED ENGINES

When I was in college I attempted a road trip with my buddy Paul. We loaded up his old VW bug to drive from Eugene, Oregon, to his home in El Paso, Texas. We made it less than a hundred miles. In the beautiful early morning light that old Volkswagen caught fire on the freeway. I still remember standing at the side of the road watching everything I own go up in flames.

And that's why I don't drive air-cooled Volkswagens.

MY TRAVELING COMPANION

Moses is a one-hundred-twenty-pound chocolate Labrador retriever and I'm his third owner. He came to me when he was eighteen months old. My ex-wife was his second owner as she had his smaller brother, Winston, who is only a hundred pounds. Moses is stronger and much more stubborn than Winston. If Moses wants to go somewhere he'll take you with him.

By the time she realized she couldn't keep him, our daughter Fiona had fallen hopelessly in love with him. Fiona worked on me for weeks telling me how I needed this dog especially since our last dogs Barney and Nina had passed away.

Finally I said she could bring him over for a weekend and we'll see. As the story goes, Fiona walked into her mother's office and said, "Dad's gonna take Moses." Her mother asked if I'd said I would. Fiona replied, "No but he said I could bring him over for a few days and we'll see."

"You're right, your Dad is taking the dog."

I'm often asked why I named him Moses and my standard reply is, "Because when he jumps into the water he parts the seas."

Truthfully Moses was the name he had when I got him and it fits. Some people like the name, others are offended by it. "How dare you name a dog after a great man in the Bible?"

I tell those people I was thinking about naming him Jesus but I already have a cat with that name.

As a traveling companion he has pluses and minuses. He rarely speaks so his conversation doesn't drive me crazy. He always lets me know when he needs to stop. He doesn't get into the other stuff in the van and he keeps his area pretty clean, even if he does shed 24/7.

On the minus side he doesn't have opposable thumbs so he can't help with the driving. His snoring has been known to wake me up both in the van and hotel rooms. And when he has running dreams he's really noisy.

He prefers sleeping on real beds whenever the opportunity arises. It's a bad habit and I shouldn't have let him get on the bed in the first place. Now it's too late to get him to change. Did I mention he's stubborn?

A dog is a great excuse to take a break. If I've been driving too long I'll stop at a rest area so we can walk around and stretch. He also comes in handy when I don't wish to go out with people after a workshop or lecture. "I have to take Moses for a walk. I'll meet you later." Then I don't.

He's always agreeable in the mornings and is rarely in a bad mood even when he hasn't had coffee. As a big dog he can be very intimidating and his bark has been known to shake windows. He's also a lovable companion who's always ready to jump in to any body of water, and that includes mud puddles.

WHEN I FIGHT AUTHORITY

Something catches my eye. I see through my side mirror a guard and his dog walk past the rear of the van. The dog stops, then starts going crazy and sniffing at the van. They slowly walk up the driver side. The guard with his extremely dark glasses stops and stares at me.

"I have a dog in the van. That's probably what he's reacting to. It's happened before."

On Interstate 10 east of El Paso there's a Border Patrol stop. It's not really on the border, in fact it's quite a few miles east of El Paso, but it's a mandatory stop that's run by the U.S. Border Patrol. Since I've never crossed the border between El Paso and Juarez I would hope there's a Border Patrol stop there as well. Maybe this one is to get the people they missed at the first one?

I'm not sure if they move it around or if it's always in the same place I just know I always have to go through it.

Today the line is long. Exhausted, I watch heavily armed agents wandering among the cars with their drug-sniffing dogs.

These agents and their dogs go through a remarkable amount of training. These dogs cannot only sniff out narcotics and humans they can also sniff out other dogs.

Every time I come through here the dogs sniff my van and start whining. The guards look at me and I calmly explain that I have another dog inside. Usually they just nod and walk off.

This guy says nothing. He continues staring at me. Finally he moves slowly past the van and I see him speak briefly into his shoulder radio. I'm screwed.

I'm on my way to Austin for a gig. I'm frazzled and I haven't slept much. Even though it's hotter than hell I have my window open and the air conditioning on full blast attempting to stay awake.

On tour I always carry my wallet on the seat next to me when I'm driving. Early on I learned that if I keep it in my pocket all day while I'm driving, my butt starts to hurt come late afternoon.

As I pull up to the front of the line, an agent checks my license plate. He asks for my driver's license. I reach over to the passenger seat...

My wallet's not there!

Fuck!

I start digging through the stuff on the passenger seat, mumbling, "It was just here." He quietly watches me.

Why do these guys all wear glasses that are so dark you can't see their eyes? Yeah I know, to intimidate you. Well right now it's working.

Finally I see my wallet lying on the floor between the two seats. I get my license out and my hands are literally shaking when I hand it to him.

"Where you headed?"

"Austin."

He hands my drivers license back.

"Would you mind pulling over there and waiting in your car?"

I feel so fucked right now.

I'm not smuggling anything. There are no drugs in the van. Hell I haven't smoked pot in thirty years.

Why am I so fucking nervous?

It's the threat that authority represents. I'm at their mercy. I'm a control freak and I don't like being at anyone's mercy! I watch movies. I know they can plant stuff on me if they don't find anything. All these scenarios flash through my exhausted brain.

I park the van where I'm told. Armed uniforms surround the van before I come to a full stop.

THE A TEAM

An agent with those goddamned dark glasses says, "Please get out of the van… slowly." He's intimidating as hell. Just like he's supposed to be.

"I have a dog in the back. He's old and probably asleep. Can I grab his leash so I can let him out?"

"Slowly."

I grab the leash. Slowly. I get out and walk around the van to the passenger side sliding door and open it. Slowly. The uniforms silently follow me. Three of them have their hands on the guns in their holsters. This is not putting me at ease.

Moses looks up as I hook the leash on him. Not that I really need to. He's eleven years old and even if he does make a break for it he won't be moving quickly.

"Step over here, sir."

They guide me to a spot some twenty feet from the van. The four of them form a circle around me. Three of them stand silently, staring at me. They still have their hands on their guns.

I want to refer to them as the A Team but I'm smart enough to know that humor is not called for at this moment.

We stop and Moses immediately lies down in the dirt and goes back to sleep. He never was much good in hot weather.

"We're going to search the van – do we have your permission?"

"There's nothing in it."

"Do we have your permission, sir?"

I don't like the way Dark Glasses is calling me "sir." Granted, I'm older than all four of them but there's something in his intonation that sounds vaguely respectful but still intimidating. It's a neat trick and it makes me feel uneasy. I wonder if they learn that in Border Patrol School?

"Sure." Like I'm gonna say no with all these guns around me.

Dark Glasses nods to an agent who is standing by the van. The agent opens all the doors.

I have visions of them throwing all my stuff on to the dirt and going through it. Then leaving it there for me to put back.

"This is your last chance to co-operate."

"Co-operate?"

"Tell us what's in the van?"

"Nothing is in the van except my travel stuff and a prescription for my asthma. Your dog smelled my dog and that's why it went crazy. It's happened before."

Dark Glasses is not buying any of this. I'm pretty sure I'm sweating at this point which is not helping my case any.

"Last chance."

"Listen, man, I'm really tired. I've been driving for three straight days and I haven't slept well these last couple nights. There is nothing in the van."

People are driving slowly by gawking out their windows as they come through the checkpoint. Here I am, surrounded by armed Border Patrol agents and my van has all of its doors open. I'm dressed in faded Levis, flip-flops and a t-shirt. Moses is sound asleep in the dirt, not a care in the world.

I'm sure these people are thinking they're witnessing a big-time bust of a notorious drug lord. Or it's just an old stoned hippie on his way home from Mexico who decided to bring some shit back with him.

Suddenly, I'm no longer nervous. What the hell? There's nothing in the van and if they say there is then I am going to ask for my one phone call and get hold of my sister. She's a retired federal prosecutor and a no-bullshit kind of person. If I tell her I've been framed she'll raise hell on my behalf ... I hope.

I wait for them to start tearing into the van. Dark Glasses continues to study me. The other agents say nothing, but they're at the ready, hands still on their guns. For some reason I want to burst out laughing. I think better of it and don't.

Finally Dark Glasses gives a signal and one of the dogs is let off the leash. It leaps into the van through the back and starts sniffing.

My first thought is, "He'd better not pee in there!"

The dog moves slowly and methodically through the mess that is the interior of the van. He stops for a moment on Moses' bed and sniffs around. Then he leaps to the front seat, sniffs, jumps out the passenger door and back to the handler. This takes less than thirty seconds but feels much longer.

The handler signals to Dark Glasses.

"There's nothing in the van."

He says this like he's surprised. Like I've ruined his day.

"I told you."

I watch as the A Team peels off and heads back to wherever they came from without a word.

I tell Mo to get up and pull on his leash. He rises slowly, shakes the dust off and we walk back to the van.

Dark Glasses walks next to me.

"I'm sorry we had to do this sir. We can't be too careful."

"It's cool. You're just doing your job."

"Really?" He seems surprised by my tone.

"Yeah. No problem." I just want to get the fuck out of here.

Moses climbs into the van, sniffs his bed for a moment, then curls up and closes his eyes.

I walk around the van closing all of the doors. Dark Glasses is still following me.

"Well, you have a nice day, sir."

"Yeah, you too."

I get in the van, start it up and as badly as I would love to say I peeled out in a cloud of dust, I slowly merge into traffic and head for Austin.

I've always had problems at government-run checkpoints. Hell, I even get hassled at the produce checkpoint at the California-Oregon border. I don't like having a bunch of heavily armed people escorting me anywhere. The TSA people never bother me at airports because as lame as some of them might be, they aren't armed.

The rest of the drive to Austin is uneventful, thank God.

Another day in the life…

THE VERY FIRST TOUR

It's dark. My eyes hurt and I think I'm in the wrong lane. I'm in heavy traffic doing sixty wondering where my exit is. There's lightning in the distance. Fuck!

I'm driving my father's pick-up truck with a canopy borrowed from my friend Richard. I bought a cheap cooler that plugs into the lighter and it's already not working.

The back of the truck is filled with over a thousand DVDs. I got printable DVDs and boxes on credit from a local company who believes in me enough to know I'll pay them back whether I sell all the DVDs or not. Another local company printed the DVD covers. A friend works there and gave me a huge discount.

My ancient HP Photosmart printed the artwork on to each DVD separately. I spent a fortune on ink cartridges, literally burning and printing DVDs one at a time for nine straight days, eighteen hours a day, before I hit the road.

I did all of my booking using a wall map of the United States I pulled out of a National Geographic magazine years ago. Where I have open days I figure I'll just wing it, maybe pick up a gig or two while I'm already out on the road. This doesn't always work.

This whole adventure starts out organized but on the day that I'm actually leaving everything dissolves into chaos. My girlfriend helps me organize and pack the truck but I have no idea what I'm going to need when. The things I need are always up by the cab. I end up re-packing the truck at least a dozen times on the road.

My plan is to be on the road by eight a.m, I don't actually hit the highway until noon.

IS THIS REALLY GOING TO WORK?

My family and friends think I'm either insane or stupid to be doing this, and many are convinced I'm going to fail. They all might be right. I spend the first night eight hours behind schedule with friends in Boise. We drink too much Sambuca and I back the truck into a mailbox trying to get it in their garage for the night. No damage, no fouls.

The following morning I feel like shit. This is not the start I imagined.

After two solid days of driving I pull into Boulder, Colorado, with twenty-three dollars in my pocket. That's not enough money for gas to get me to my next stop, or to get home. If I don't make money here the tour is over before it even begins.

My first stop is the university where I'm doing a guest lecture for the princely sum of seventy-five dollars. Which, of course, they won't pay me until thirty days after I've invoiced them. A fact I'm not aware of. Yet.

It doesn't go well. I'm sure I'm funny and informative and I'm passing on real-world experience. The students appear less than impressed. I manage to sell two DVDs and make twenty dollars.

I meet as many faculty members as I can to see if anyone else wants me to do a guest lecture while I'm here. No takers. Some of the faculty are quite rude. Have they already heard my first lecture was less than successful?

It dawns on me slowly. Why in the world would I think that any of these professors would want me to talk about filmmaking and show my work? They're academics and obviously know more about filmmaking than I do. I'm merely a working filmmaker.

Maybe this tour wasn't a good idea...

WARNING: ADULT CONTENT

The next morning I do a workshop at a private media company that's paying me a large sum of money to speak to their employees about sound and my experiences making films.

The employee who set up the gig is letting me stay at his house and picking up all my meals. He'd gone to the university and his mentor was Stan Brakhage. I'm a huge fan of Brakhage. We have some great conversations, as he's a gifted filmmaker in his own right.

Did I forget to mention that the media company is a cable channel that specializes in "adult content," delivered discreetly to your hotel room?

They don't make the porn. They just edit trailers, teasers and other promotional stuff for the porn. Many of the employees I meet are graduates of the university's film program.

Most of them are working on their own films – animated, experimental, and independent – outside of their jobs. I'm told that if you graduate from Boulder with a film degree and you want to stay in the area, your choices are working for the Ski Film King (who apparently doesn't pay shit – that's just what I heard) or you can work for this porn comp... I mean, media company, that does pay well.

Since they all have student loans and staying in Boulder isn't cheap, they work where they work.

As you can imagine it takes a while to get used to talking to a room full of people as muted hardcore porn plays on the monitor in the back of the conference room, which of course I'm facing. I'm doing my best to act casual and pretend that it's no big deal. I just need to focus on what I'm talking about and not wonder how that couple on TV got into that position?

They turn out to be a great audience! Their questions are well thought out and they take notes like crazy while I explain how I solve particular problems on the various films I've worked on.

Three hours flew by and after a wonderful catered lunch they line up to buy my films like there was no tomorrow.

I receive my check as soon as the workshop is over. I love these guys!

The tour will go on.

After this gig I start doing something that I continue to do to this day. I figure out how much money I need for my next couple stops and then I send all the checks and most of the money I make on merchandise home to be deposited into an account that I don't have easy access to.

If I only have a small amount of money on me then I'm going to work hard at every gig. It's great motivation to do the best workshop or guest lecture I can. If audiences are actively engaged then most of them will buy a DVD, book or a T-shirt afterward.

IT WAS A DARK AND STORMY NIGHT...

Pulling into Huntington, West Virginia, late one night, the clouds open up. I finally find the hotel I'm supposed to be staying at. It's dark and deserted and looks like something out of a Roger Corman monster movie. And it's locked.

I find the local community theater, where I'm scheduled to speak the next day. I ask around to see if anyone knows about the people I'm supposed to meet.

I'm given directions to a house on the hill where the hotel

owner lives. I'm not feeling good about this. I forgot to pack a coat so now I'm soaked and freezing. I finally find the house.
I'm told everyone's at a roadhouse out on the highway and two people I've never met offer to take me out there, and says one, "So you can get in."

So I can get in? What the fuck?

It's a private roadhouse.

We pull up next to a beat-up trailer, I mean "manufactured home," sitting literally on the shoulder of the road with a bunch of cars parked around it. To this day in my mind I'm convinced it's leaning to one side. We approach a locked door that has a 1970s-era security camera perched above it. A button is pushed, my new friends tell the scratchy, distorted voice coming from the ancient speaker who we are.

The door clicks open...

Isn't this how horror movies start? Will there be people in hockey masks or guys saying, "Squeal like a pig," when I enter?

Hey, where's your sense of adventure?

The group from the Filmmakers Guild is here. A cold beer is immediately thrust into my hand and I'm welcomed with open arms and mass quantities of alcohol.

By the time we got back to the Horror Hotel it's really late. I'm feeling no pain but I'm still wet and cold. I don't believe that roadhouses have heat.

The owner is renovating the hotel and that's why it looks the way it does. The one floor we're all staying on is very nice. I soon find my room and a bed. I sleep like shit because I can't get warm. I shiver under the single blanket all night.

The next morning, fuck, I'm sick. I didn't get sick, and I'm not hung over. I have a full-blown cold. I need coffee, drugs, a hot shower and more sleep. Not necessarily in that order.

Stumbling around town looking for coffee, I find the only place that's open: a tiny bar. It's eight o'clock in the morning and the bar is full of grizzled old men drinking beer and chain smoking. You can tell these guys have worked hard and lived hard, you can see it in their tired worn faces. And I wouldn't mess with any of them.

It's a no-frills kind of place. No food, just cases of beer that are being served out of coolers. Forget glasses, we're talking straight out of the can.

The bartender apologizes for not having any coffee made but this is not a morning coffee crowd. She makes a pot just for me. While I wait I'm convinced I'm going to choke to death on the cigarette smoke.

Everyone's staring at me because obviously I'm not a local. Finally I have a cup of steaming hot liquid in a tiny Styrofoam cup. I have no idea what kind of coffee it is and I don't care. It burns my throat as well as my hands.

My lungs are aching from the thick smoke. Did I mention I'm asthmatic?

I down a second cup of "coffee" and get the hell out of there. I'm feeling worse and I'm having difficulty breathing.

But the show must go on!

I'm able to rally enough strength to do my workshop. Everyone's happy and impressed. I'm impressed that I haven't hacked up a lung.

I spend one more night wearing two sets of clothes in my drafty hotel room and wake up even sicker. It doesn't matter. I'm off to my next stop, Philadelphia.

I stop in rest areas along the way and try to get a little sleep. My head is pounding, I'm sweating profusely, and I'm having a tough time just breathing. Add in some East Coast humidity and lots of traffic and you get the picture.

BETTER LIVING THROUGH CHEMISTRY

From the road I call Rob, the fellow I'm staying with in Philadelphia and ask about pharmacies close to his house. I call my doctor in Portland and describe my symptoms. His fear is bronchitis so he faxes a bunch of prescriptions to a pharmacy near Rob's house.

He tells me I need rest and shouldn't move around for a couple days. Like that's gonna happen.

I arrive at the pharmacy as they're filling my prescriptions. I start taking pills on the spot, without water. I have a three-hour workshop the next day and I feel like I've been run over by a truck.

I finally get to Rob's house. One look at me and I'm sure he's convinced I'm gonna die on him.

The next morning I'm still feeling weak but I've got a show to do.

The meds are slowly kicking in but my breathing is still labored. The day is going to be hot and humid. Let's face it, any humidity is tough on us West Coast guys. I'm sweating bullets just walking from the house to the car.

My workshop is being held on the third floor of an old building without air conditioning and, of course, no elevator. I trudge up the stairs stopping every now and again attempting to catch my breath. My breathing is quite audible. My lungs sound like there's a baby rattle stuck way down inside.

Ordinarily when I teach I'm on my feet, constantly moving, like a shark. I've learned it's harder to hit a moving target. But on this miserable day in Philadelphia I sit for the entire workshop. I'm convinced my lungs are going to seize up and my head's going to explode sending millions of screaming brain cells across the room.

I go through all of the material but I'm convinced I'm not entertaining enough. Which is a problem I have after almost every workshop or lecture. "Why didn't they laugh at this point? A few people looked bored?" I know I'm harder on myself than any of my audiences will ever be. It's that fucked-up need for approval we all have. Even though the group assures me the workshop was great, it doesn't make me feel better. I need more therapy.

We go back to Rob's house where I take more drugs and sleep. Later that night I'm feeling a little better so we go out for a cheese steak because that's what you do in Philadelphia.

We go to Pat's, and Rob instructs me on the proper way to order. I order a "cheese steak *wit*." I don't remember what that means but it was good. I ask if the place across the street, Gino's, is any good. Rob says he doesn't know, he's never tried it. Never tried it? It's right across the street!

Rob informs me that you either go to Pat's or to Gino's, but no one goes to both. You're a fan of one or the other. Go figure. Must be a Philly thing.

I leave the following day, stopping every couple hours and trying to sleep in humid, noisy rest areas. Why do I always park next to screaming noisy kids or rumbling semis?

Being sick is no fun. Being sick on the road by yourself is its own special hell!

HOTEL DESK CLERK FROM HELL

I swing through Chicago where I'm set to do a guest lecture at Columbia College and talk to some classes. I'm booked at a hotel a block away and Columbia is taking care of everything.

The hotel garage is closed for some dumb reason, so I can't park there. I still have a lot of stuff in the back and I don't want anyone to break into the canopy. Actually I don't want anyone to break the canopy trying to steal a bunch of DVDs they won't even want. It's not my canopy.

I look for a garage and navigate traffic as a Bears game is ending. Yes, my hotel is right down the street from the stadium. I finally find a secure garage a few blocks away and get my truck in without running over anyone. If I had run over anyone it would've been justified – these people are fucking rude!

Back at the hotel, Donny the desk clerk wants an imprint of my credit card. I only have a debit card and the college is picking up everything. I'm told they need it in case I use the phone. I show him my cell. The mini bar? I don't want the key to it. He persists.

I tell him the reason I don't want him to swipe my card is that I've just paid my bills and I barely have enough to cover them. If they put a hold on the card I'll bounce a check. "Can you give me a break?"

Donny assures me he'll just swipe the card so they have a record of the number in case I do use it for something. Nothing will be charged on it until I check out and then I'll be notified. We go back and forth on this. Against my better judgment I let him take the card.

At Columbia my lecture is in their brand new theater that's only used for special guests. I have to ask, "Who was here last?" Henry Fucking Rollins! Damn I'm in good company!

It's a great couple days and when I check out I'm assured that nothing is put on my debit card.

I somehow manage to finish the tour and make it home in one

piece. Going through my mail I come across a bounced check notification from my bank. Then another from my mortgage company! I was in arrears and the check I had written them covered everything and should have gotten me current. And it bounced. What the fuck?

There's also a letter saying they're going to commence with foreclosure proceedings.

Since this was before the days of having access to your bank account online I had to wait until the next day to go to the bank. The teller looks it up and sure enough the hotel in Chicago not only charged my debit card, they charged it for my entire stay! I'm pissed. I call the hotel and finally someone sees that I've been charged for the room, and Columbia paid for it as well.

I'm already steamed and then they tell me it'll take up to three business days to reverse the charges. I call the mortgage company and am told, "Tough luck." They're moving ahead with foreclosure proceedings. And they've added a bunch of fees on top of what I owed them on the back payments.

I'm not at all surprised during the great Depression of the 1930s that people were shooting bankers. Many of them are sleazy motherfuckers, as we know from our most recent recession.

After a long horrible conversation with my lawyer we come to the conclusion that the best thing I can do is sell my house and pay everybody and everything off and start from scratch. (At the time I was heavily in debt to the IRS because of one of my films, but that's a story for another time…)

So I sell my home of twenty years.

And I'll never forget the name of the hotel, which no longer exists, and that asshole Donny who lied to me and ran my debit card.

So now that I no longer have a home I might as well spend more time out on the road.

MY OTHER TRAVELING COMPANION

I bought a used 2005 Ford Freestar with nine thousand miles on it. I had a roof rack installed and I carry two Thule boxes up top.

I removed the middle seat the day I bought it (it's still in storage) and I take out the rear seat when I'm on the road. My friend Richard built a wooden platform that's half the width of the van and goes from the tailgate to the back of the driver seat. It sits twenty inches off the floor and has a hinged top for easy access to the things I store underneath. I sleep on the platform when I don't have lodging or don't want to pay for it.

Moses' bed is behind the front passenger seat so I can look over and see he's okay at any time. His food and water bowls fit next to his bed and after a few days he perfected the art of eating and drinking while lying down.

The van is filled with plastic containers that hold all of my merchandise; DVDs, CDs, books, T-shirts, posters, and office supplies. I have one container for food as well as paper plates, utensils, and a container that holds forty pounds of dry dog food. I carry a couple gallons of drinking water, a pillow, a sleeping bag, an air mattress, and a lantern.

I have two duffel bags with enough clothes in each to last ten days. When it's time to switch bags I have ten days to find a place to do laundry, which is usually people's homes.

In the back is a large fishing cooler full of fruit, vegetables, cheeses, and deli meats. I don't eat out much – it gets expensive and after a while all restaurant food tastes the same. Plus, I'm already a good-sized guy and if I eat fast food or in restaurants for two months by the time I get home I'm going to be huge.

Fully loaded the van gets around twenty miles per gallon. As the tour progresses the van gets lighter and the gas mileage gets better, but not all that much. The gas tank holds around twenty-five gallons, which is good for over four hundred miles on a single fill up. With gas prices fluctuating there have been times its cost me almost a hundred dollars to fill it up. That's ten DVDs or five t-shirts I need to sell.

All maintenance is done regularly, especially oil changes. I'm lucky enough to say (knock on wood) that I have never been stranded or needed a tow. Take care of your car and it will take care of you.

The van is great for stealth camping as it has tinted windows.

I pull into motel parking lots early in the morning to use their wifi for emails. Sometimes I walk in and enjoy the "free continental breakfast." If you walk in with confidence they don't question you, especially if you ask, "What time is check out?"

The touring life is really an extension of what I've been doing for years.

Living in Portland I realized that if I wanted to have a career doing what I love then I was going to have to travel. I've never been able make a living just working in town. The filmmakers I know who always work don't rely on Portland or even Oregon for their income. They're working all over the country. The road life is a necessity, I suppose.

There's a huge difference in traveling for work and going out on tour. You have different stresses and needs. Most people who travel for work fly and stay in hotels. This kind of travel is all about the destination. If I'm flying, I can have a bag packed and be out the door in twenty minutes. You work on the airplane and at thirty-five thousand feet there isn't all that much to see. Airports are always a hassle. You've got crowds, security, and if you have to change planes you rarely have time to get from one gate to the next because the gates you need are never close to each other.

Add in flights being late, getting a rental car, finding your way to the hotel, and settling in to a fairly sterile room. Your days are usually set up around meetings and getting things accomplished. And it's always a rush to get back to the airport so that you don't miss your late-night flight home.

There are times you're stranded in an airport because of weather or missed connections or a problem with the plane. I've slept overnight on the floor of more than a few airports waiting for that early morning flight back home.

Basically, business travel can suck!

Going on the road for two months requires a different kind of planning. As a one-person operation, I'm taking care of everything and that always starts at least a couple months before I hit the road.

Booking all of the gigs and finding the most efficient ways to get from one booking to the next. There are always traffic jams to be anticipated and the great unknowns that are weather and road construction. Am I staying in hotels, with friends, or sleeping in the van? I do all the publicity, which means contacting newspapers and anyone else I think can help publicize my event.

Preparing the van requires getting the maintenance done, getting all of the DVDs and other merchandise I'm going to need as well as buying food. I pack the van as efficiently as possible, which means I'm always loading it late the night before I hit the road.

Unlike flying, road trips are as much about the journey as they are about the destination.

There is something romantic about being on the road. We read about it and want to live vicariously imagining what life out there is like. After all these years of being on the road I can honestly say that it is romantic and an adventure. It's also boring, monotonous, and scary.

Did I mention I'm addicted?

BAD DAD

Fiona's mad at me.

There's nothing worse than your eleven-year-old daughter not talking to you. I'm the worst dad in the world. I try to explain things to her and most of the time she gets it. This is one of those times when she doesn't.

I'm going to miss the school play she's in. In my defense she hadn't tried out for the play until I was already on the road. Hell, when I left I didn't even know there was going to be a school play.

At first she said it wasn't a big deal and it's okay that I'm not there. Apparently that has now changed. The play is on Saturday. It's Wednesday.

I can't drop everything and grab a flight to Portland. I can't afford it and even if I could, I'm booked on Friday and Saturday.

She won't talk to me.

Ordinarily Fiona and I talk every other day. She tells me what's going on and I tell her what Moses and I have done. Now she won't tell me anything. I try to reason with her but you can't reason with a seventh grader. I should know better.

I miss the show and I feel rotten. She's still mad and for two weeks won't talk. She's very short on the phone and then says she has to go.

I hate being frozen out like this.

I tell her I feel bad about missing the show but I did and I can't make that up. She's being unresponsive and ready to hang up. I'm two thousand miles away working my ass off and I can't take it anymore.

"You know Fiona, this hurts me too. I wish I could have been there and at the time you said it wasn't important and then it became important and I couldn't get there because of previous commitments."

"I know. I have to go."

"Listen to me because I'm only going to say this once and then I'm done. I've never missed any of your school stuff. Usually I'm the only dad there, but I've never missed anything starting with pre-school. Yes, I feel like shit for missing the play and you're making me feel worse. You're also being unfair and unreasonable. You never told me the play was important to you until it was too late and I couldn't do anything about it. I already had bookings that I couldn't re-schedule. You can hate me if you wish but you need to know how much your behavior is hurting me. Now you can hang up if you want to..."

And she does.

I look at Moses and shrug. I get the feeling he understands. I need to go teach a workshop.

The next day she calls.

"Dad, I'm sorry. I was just really hurt and I shouldn't take it out on you. I know you're doing your best and you're right, you've never missed any of my other school stuff. Can we start over?"

I felt a huge sense of relief. A weight being lifted from my shoulders. "Absolutely!"

I HAVE TWO LEFT FEET

I'm still touring when Fiona goes to high school. She's at an all-girls school and every fall they have a Father-Daughter Dance the first weekend in October.

For four years no matter where I'm at I always clear out the first weekend of October for the Father-Daughter Dance at Fiona's school. It's not always easy getting back to Portland for the dance. I have to be near an airport, find a place to park the van where it won't be vandalized and, most importantly, find someone I trust to take care of Moses for the short time I'm gone.

Anyone who knows me knows I don't like dances. I love music, it's a big part of my life, but I can't sing and I certainly can't dance. I'm extremely self-conscious, I feel like I look like an idiot, and I have no rhythm. But other than that…

I never learned how to dance. You would think that after all these years I would have gotten over this but I haven't. I'm intimidated on the dance floor. I'm convinced everyone is watching me and realizing that I'm faking it. I go to great lengths to avoid going anywhere there is dancing. And yet here I am.

At our first dance Fiona says, "Mom said you don't dance and all the years you were together you only danced with her a couple times. That's okay if you don't want to dance. I'm just glad you're here."

I feel as though my ex-wife just threw down the gauntlet. I will not disappoint my daughter. "Come on." Fiona and I get out on the dance floor and I do my best for a bunch of songs. I'm sweating profusely when I finally say, "Uncle."

As we walk back to our table I say, "I just danced more with you right now than I ever did with your mother the whole time we were together."

"Cool!"

I don't tell her that I still feel like an idiot and I'm pretty sure everyone can tell I have no rhythm. But I did it.

At the dance her senior year, she and the other senior girls had to give one minute speeches about their fathers. This is the speech Fiona gave:

Dad, I would like to thank you for the following things:

1. For teaching me all of the words to I Am The Walrus before I learned that the alphabet did not end with W.
2. For introducing me to punk rock at the tender age of eight and making me the social leper of Mrs. Johnson's third-grade class.
3. For taking me to Dairy Queen on a bad day.
4. For taking me to Dairy Queen on a good day.
5. For taking me to Diary Queen on any day that ends with "y."
6. For weaving all sorts of obscure pop culture references into my life that my friends have learned to stop asking me about. "Danger Will Robinson!"
7. For planting in my heart a deep hatred for Led Zeppelin and all things Star Wars making me instantly undateable to every teenage boy ever. Thanks.
8. For deciding it was okay to name me Fiona rather than Madame Curie or Ginger like you really wanted to.
9. For flying across the country every year for four years to sit through speeches exactly like this one.
10. And lastly for always supporting me and being my biggest fan no matter what Mom or my college counselor says about it being a bad idea to run away to Argentina and become a tango dancer.

After this speech I had a lot of fathers come up to me and tell me what a cool kid I have. I agree.

After the dance we get ice cream, then head home and talk late into the night. She catches me up with her life in a few short hours. I make breakfast the next morning and take her to school. Then it's time for me to fly back to where Moses and the van are waiting.

There's always a time change involved and even though I'm home for less than thirty hours, I'm exhausted for days. The short trip home is always brutal. But I never missed a dance and I always danced with Fiona. Every year she lets me know how much it means to her that I'm there at the dance.

WACO IS A LONG WAY FROM ANYWHERE

Fiona calls to tell me that her high school is having its one-hundred-fiftieth birthday celebration at one of the big concert halls in town. She's in the show as part of the choir. I'm so proud.

"Do you want me there?"

"No, it's okay, Dad. You're working."

"You're sure. I don't want to have problems again."

"No, it's no big deal. Plus even though the tickets are free they've all been given out."

"Okay. If it becomes important will you tell me?"

"I will."

The next day my phone rings.

"Is there any way you can make it back for my school's celebration?"

"I thought it wasn't important."

"It is."

"Then I'll be there. How can I get a ticket?"

"My friend's mom has an extra one. She said I could have it."

"How will I get it?"

"We'll work that out."

Oh fuck!

Three days before the event I'm at Baylor in Waco, Texas. I could do two more gigs on my way home. Screw that, I call and cancel both. They weren't in stone anyway.

The most direct route would be to drive through Denver, then Salt Lake City to Portland. It's still snowing up there and the weather is unpredictable. I need to stay south for as long as possible.

I can drive through Texas to New Mexico, then Arizona, and California. I can avoid the traffic in Los Angeles if I cut up through Bakersfield, then over to Interstate 5 and straight up to Portland.

Twenty-four-hundred miles and it should take about forty hours. I have less than three days.

I go out for BBQ that night. I eat too much and get sick. I toss and turn trying to sleep. My alarm goes off at six a.m. It's not pretty. I load the van and Moses and I are on the road by seven.

The first day is miserable. I feel like shit. Luckily there's not much traffic and I'm smart enough to stay within the speed limit. I make it to Los Cruces late the first night and I'm spent. I'm not sure how I'm gonna pull this off.

I sleep surprisingly well in a Walmart parking lot as semis scream by on the highway. My alarm jolts me awake at five a.m. It's below freezing as Moses and I walk around the parking lot. I'm shivering and naturally he's in no hurry. I think his goal is to mark as many places as he can. My goal is to avoid frostbite. I suppose I should be wearing socks and more than a thin tattered sweatshirt but it was a lot warmer when we left Waco.

With no gloves and no ice scraper I scrape the ice off my windshield with my library card. The defroster is blowing nothing but cold air. My teeth are chattering. The highway is pitch black as we pull out. It's no one but me and the semis.

Heading west I know I'll gain another hour, which I'll put to good use behind the wheel.

I drive nineteen hours through New Mexico, Arizona and into California. I stick to two-lane highways so I can avoid Los Angeles entirely. Going through Bakersfield is never pretty and a strong northerly wind hits us as I finally merge on to I-5. I make it just past Sacramento before I finally pull over at a rest stop. I can hardly keep my eyes open and it's still windy as hell. My shoulders and neck hurt as I crawl into the back of the van to get some sleep. I'm so tired I don't lay out my air mattress. I crawl full clothed into my sleeping bag. The van shakes all night and I can hear branches cracking and breaking, but it's not the worst sleep I've ever had.

I wake up as it gets light. The wind is gone. I feel surprisingly well.

I've got about six hundred miles and the concert starts at seven. I think I can make it. My plan is to swing by the house, drop off the dog, take a shower, and change clothes as I'm still wearing the same ones I put on in Waco.

The last day of driving is sunny and warm. I zip up I-5 and make it to Portland with two hours to spare.

I go home and get that shower I've been dying for. Moses is happily sniffing around the patio to make sure no one has trespassed on his turf. I jump into my other car and even though it's been sitting for two months, it starts right up.

I'm standing in front of the venue at quarter till seven. I'm starving and tired and my body still feels like I'm moving. I meet up with Fiona's friend's mom and get my ticket.

The concert is wonderful even though Fiona and the choir only sing a couple songs over an hour and a half. The concert hall is packed with alumni who know all the words to the school song and belt it out with emotion and enthusiasm. Hell, I don't know if my high school even had a song.

Afterwards I meet Fiona out front. She gives me a huge hug.

We go get Mexican food and after one of the toughest drives I've ever done I realize, maybe I'm not such a bad dad after all.

NAMING the TOURS and OTHER LESS THAN STELLAR IDEAS

There was a time when some friends and I decided we should name my different tours. Bands do it all the time and I was thinking this would be a way to differentiate the tours. There was also some thought given to designing special posters and T-shirts for each individual tour.

Then I found out how much it would cost to make up special posters and T-shirts. Even if I sold them all, I'd still have to front the money to make everything and my budget for the tours is pretty much non-existent since I already pay for all of the DVDs, books, and the regular Angry Filmmaker T-shirts. So that idea was out.

Still some friends and I came up with tour names and I even asked some of my followers. We gave out a prize for the best name. The prize was copies of my films.

Here are some of the titles:

- The Anger Management Tour
- AngryFilmmakerpolooza
- The IRS Tour
- The Hollywood is Dead Tour
- Let's Get Angry Tour
- Compromise Kills
- A man. His dog. A van. Some films.
- Never Mind Sundance: It's the Angry Filmmaker
- Anger to the People
- Angry Filmmaking 101 Tour
- The "Screw Distribution! Let's Tour!" Tour
- Get Your Own Damn Tour!
- I Sold Out to Hollywood and All I Got Was This Lousy T-shirt!
- The Angry Filmmaker's Make a Left at Albuquerque Tour
- Angry Across America
- They Loved Him in Minneapolis Tour
- Frankly, America, I Don't Give a Damn
- Grass Roots. Brass Knuckles: The Angry Filmmaker Tour
- The Kicking & Screaming Tour
- The Angry Filmmaker's Hollywood-Schmollywood Tour
- The F@#* Hollywood Tour

As I recall the winner of our one and only contest was Jim Dougherty for his entry, The Angry Filmmaker's Au-Tour. (I hope you're still enjoying those DVDs, Jim.)

But my favorite tour name, complete with poster, came from Bill Dever. He and I were talking about the tour and tour names and other stuff. A couple days later he emails me a poster with a drawing of Moses on it and the words: *The Moses Tour (featuring The Guy Who Feeds Me)*. Thanks, Bill.

Another marketing suggestion was that people could sign up to win a date or dinner with The Angry Filmmaker while I was out on tour. That idea obviously came from someone who had never been out on the road and seen the type of people that I draw to my events. I vetoed this one.

People would suggest that I shoot video of my tours and while I was on the road do a quick edit and upload these pieces to my website as well as some social media sites.

A great idea if it weren't for the fact that I'm speaking, teaching, screening, judging and *driving* almost every day. Where would I get the time to do this? People don't understand that touring is more than a full-time job.

YOU ARE NOT ORIGINAL! BUT NEITHER AM I.

This subject came up much more frequently after I started reading about this filmmaker who was touring with a couple other filmmakers. They were doing these "crazy" things on the road and posting them up on to the Internet. Mostly they appeared to be drinking and laughing a lot. I do remember one where they were trying to get invited to someone's set or something so it was lots of phone calls in motel rooms and laughing and drinking. Or something like that.

A couple writers picked up on this and wrote some articles about how new and cool this was, taking your films out on tour. Like it had never been done before. I got pissed and perhaps a bit jealous because I'd already been touring for a few years and, let's face it, I can be as shallow as the next guy.

I politely responded to one article (in the comments section) saying film tours were nothing new and had been going on since the invention of the medium. Producers and other hucksters would bring their films to your town for one night only. In the early days it was almost like the circus or a carnival coming to town. These people would rent a hall, charge admission and for one or two nights only would show the most recent wonders on film. It was things like a train coming toward the audience, news events, and things of that nature.

In the 1950s some producers brought low-budget horror films to small towns and would promote them saying things like people had heart attacks during the screening because it's so scary, or it's so horrible that we'll be giving out "throw-up" bags to all of the customers. They'd say whatever they thought it would take to get people in the door.

And I pointed out that there were other filmmakers on tour at this moment who had been doing it for years. What these guys were doing was not original and it was annoying to me that they were appearing to take credit for this "new type of distribution."

I got a nice response from one writer who acknowledged on his site that what I said was true. It was obvious that he'd taken the time to look me up before he responded. As I recall he mentioned in his response in the comments thread that I'd been touring for years.

Sometime later I show up at a conference where I'm speaking. My friend Joe grabs me and takes me to a session where this same "touring" filmmaker and his editor were talking about self-distribution (or something). The session was in progress and there wasn't a huge group of people in the room so when we walked in everyone turned around. Joe and I quietly sat at the back. This filmmaker looked at me and I think he knew who I was.

Long story short: Within a short time of our entrance he excused himself to go to another engagement and walked out before his session was over leaving the other fellow to take questions. Which is certainly tacky behavior as far as I'm concerned. These people came to hear him speak.

When the questions start one person asks something the editor doesn't know the answer to. My friend Joe speaks up and says that I could answer that question as I've been touring for years. All eyes turn to the back of the room. So I answer the question. Then more questions came my way. I answered them all as best

I could. When the session was over even though I was just a spectator I was surrounded by filmmakers asking me questions.

I never did get a chance to meet that other filmmaker. Apparently he left the conference a short time later.

It seems like all the ideas that people came up with for me to do on tour required a lot more work than I can do. On the road I have a tough time just keeping up on Twitter and Facebook, how the hell can I do all this other stuff?

Maybe one day Moses and I can tour with a whole crew on our own tour bus. Or even just a small motor home.

It's good to have a dream.

LONGEST SOLO DRIVE EVER

I'm going well over ninety when I see a Texas State Trooper pass me on the other side of the highway heading west. No worries. He can't tell how fast I'm going.

Can he?

A few minutes later I see him flying up behind me with lights flashing.

A lot of people think West Texas is flat and boring. I don't. I come from a state that can feel too green, with too many hills. When you're driving in the Northwest for hours it gets monotonous in a different way. You feel like you're driving a lot but not getting anywhere. All the ups and downs and twists and turns and with the hills surrounding you, you don't get any feeling of forward motion. You have so many trees on either side of the highway that you have no point of reference. It's also really hard to make good time when you're constantly slowing down for sharp turns. And don't get me started about the slow Oregon drivers.

The great thing about West Texas is the speed limit. Eighty-miles-per-hour. West Texas is wide open and besides semis there's never much traffic to speak of.

Even though the van has cruise control I never use it. It makes me feel like I'm not totally in control of the vehicle. I fear that the less I do while driving the greater the chance I will space out and fuck up. Hell, I don't even like driving an automatic but I couldn't find a van with a manual. Except VWs and you know how I feel about those.

My rule of thumb is keep it under ten miles an hour over the speed limit if you want to avoid a ticket. So eighty-five to eighty-eight miles an hour should keep me under any cops radar and there are very few cops out here anyway.

I really suck at judging distances, which explains why I need to drive eighteen hours today.

This leg of the tour started in Phoenix on a Thursday. I'd foolishly booked an all day workshop in Houston on Saturday. As I've often done, I booked these workshops using the map in my head. The map in my head said the whole drive should take maybe twelve hours.

The real map said it was almost twelve hundred miles, an eighteen-hour drive. And that's if I do it non-stop.

Confident in my driving abilities, I pull out of Phoenix at five a.m. on five hours sleep. It's pitch black and I have to navigate some tiny two-lane roads to get to the highway.

The drive is going well and I can feel my foot pushing down on the accelerator more and more. It's already a long day and I need to make better time.

And that's when it happens…

This State Trooper doesn't appear to be in a good mood when he comes up to my window and tells me to get out. Slowly…

"Yes sir." And I keep my hands where he can see them at all times.

I'm always polite when I deal with law enforcement. It's a shitty job and I certainly wouldn't want to do it. I've learned that if you're polite and respectful they might let you off with a warning. But most important of all is there's an awful lot of places in west Texas you can dump a body and it'll never be found. This guy probably knows them all.

I get out slowly, and walk around to the passenger side of the van. He orders me to put my hands on my head, which I do.

"Where are you going and what's in the van?"

I tell him, and say if he wants to open the sliding door to check it out, and he's more than welcome to, please be careful of Moses, who's probably sleeping. I assure him Moses is big but very gentle. I continue to be polite and respectful, always calling him "sir."

He's a total dick.

He says some rude and condescending things as he takes my license and registration.

I don't know what comes over me as he's armed and I'm not. I look him in the eye, or where his eyes would be if he wasn't wearing those damn mirrored shades and ask if I've insulted him or said something disrespectful? He says nothing. I tell him I hope not and I know that he's doing his job but I would appreciate being treated with the same respect I'm showing him.

He says nothing as he goes to his car to check me out. What am I thinking? Here I am with my hands on my head standing on the side of a lonely stretch of highway. I haven't seen another car pass by this whole time. I'm buzzard food.

When he comes back he's a bit more polite but still a dick. He doesn't give me a ticket although he gives me a written warning.

"It's gonna be dark in a few hours and you need to slow down. I've called your license plate in and if you're caught speeding or doing anything else illegal today then you'll be getting a ticket and possibly going to jail."

Jail? For what? I decide against asking as I feel I've already pushed my luck with this guy.

And you know what? I get it. These guys have a tough job and they meet a lot of people who say shitty things to them. It's too bad that this guy felt like he had to continue to act like a dick. At least I don't get a ticket.

"Thank you. Have a nice day!" I say as I slowly walk back to my van.

Why the fuck am I so polite? I blame my parents. I was raised to always be polite and respectful of others. Sometimes I really hate that about myself.

I drive down the road and suddenly realize I'm exhausted. I've been driving for eleven hours and still have a long way to go. I pull into the first rest area I find, tilt the seat back and take a thirty-minute nap. I wake up semi-refreshed and sweating like a pig. I left my windows open while I slept, as I didn't want to leave the van running and the air conditioning on. It's sweltering and I've been joined in the van by an amazing array of bugs.

Yeah I know, I'm in Texas. What'd I expect?

I walk Moses around the rest area so he can do his business, I eat a piece of fruit and some trail mix, and off we go.

I keep telling myself Houston is doable. I also don't have a choice, as the workshop is an all-day affair starting at nine a.m.

I have to keep going. I can't stop for the night and get up early, if I hit any traffic problems early in the morning I'm fucked. Besides my room in Houston is paid for and I'm too cheap to rent another one.

The sun goes down.

I fall in behind a semi that's making good time, even with the reduced speed limit. I hope he's going to Houston.

Driving behind the semi I'm not worried about all the deer I'm seeing at the side of the road. If they do choose to end it all, the semi will no doubt accommodate them much more thoroughly than I can and probably with less front-end damage. I'm close enough that there isn't much room for a deer to leap between us, but back far enough so that he knows I'm here.

You never want to piss off truck drivers, especially late at night on dark highways. Think about it…

I'm eating trail mix as I drive. I'm hungry but I don't want to stop and grab a meal. I have this dumb idea that eating trail mix is healthier than stopping for fast food. I'm also using the sugar in the chocolate chips and M&Ms to keep me going. It's not much but it's all I got.

I follow this truck until well after midnight. He pulls off in some nameless town in the middle of nowhere. I'm still a couple hours from Houston. Which sounds like a good name for a country song.

Truck drivers are only allowed a certain amount of time behind the wheel before they're required to stop. I realize how smart this is because I'm beyond exhausted. I barrel through the black Texas night.

I'm pretty sure I'm not hallucinating when I finally pull into Houston around three a.m. My GPS is working great and I can see my hotel from the freeway. Then I notice the exit is closed. Construction. Houston is alive with nighttime construction and it's centered around my hotel.

I drive in circles for forty-five minutes trying to get to the hotel. On the freeway. Off the freeway. Down side streets. Making U-turns. Cutting across parking lots. Now I think I'm hallucinating and I'm sure the gods are laughing at me in my sorry state.

I finally pull into the hotel and park in a thirty-minute zone out front. There are no parking attendants, bellhops, or anyone else for that matter. I grab my duffel bag. Moses follows me as I stagger into the lobby.

I think I had a nice conversation with the desk clerk, but I don't remember. I probably appear absolutely deranged, as I'm so frustrated with all of the construction and the fact that I've just driven over twenty straight hours, with only a thirty-minute nap.

I get up to the room and suddenly all of the trail mix I've been eating for the last eight hours catches up to me. I make it to the bathroom in the nick of time. I'm convinced that half my insides come out my ass in a few wretched moments.

I stagger into the bedroom and there's Moses loudly snoring on one of the two queen size beds. Nothing fazes him.

The seven-thirty wake up call jolts me out of bed. God only knows what I say to the operator in my incoherent state but the call gets me up and into the shower.

I make it to the theater just in time. Michelle, who booked this gig, knows I'm running on just a couple hours' sleep and keeps me supplied with hi-test coffee all day.

I'm not sure how I pull it off, but I do. The students learn a lot about sound design, so SWAMP (Southwest Alternative Media Project) is happy. I get paid so I'm happy. I pass on dinner with friends and go back to the hotel. I sleep for twelve hours. I'm up early the next morning, load the van and on to my next destination.

I wish I could say that after this experience I always consult a real map before I book my tours. But I don't. Luckily I've never driven that far again in a single day.

FILM FESTIVALS are HARD WORK

"Hi. Remember me? I'm the guy with the fiancée with the huge boobs."

At one festival I meet a leather-clad, tattooed, and pierced web developer from Chicago. He's there with his girlfriend who's also tattooed, pierced and in leather. Their favorite films are the schlocky horror films from the sixties and seventies so they're having a great time at this festival. I spend a lot of time talking with them, as they're smart and interesting.

Yes, his fiancée does have "huge boobs," that's obvious. But he's making the assumption that he's forgettable or that all I'm focused on are her boobs, which is incorrect. Maybe I'm the exception but I remember talking to both of them and not just staring at her chest.

The next day he comes up and re-introduces himself, like I wouldn't remember him with all of his tattoos, piercings and, yes, he's still dressed all in leather. "Remember me? We talked yesterday. I'm the guy with the fiancée with the huge boobs."

We corresponded for a while and every time I got an email from him he always started it off with, "Remember me. I'm the guy with the fiancée with the huge boobs."

No, you're the guy with the self-esteem issues.

On tour I book as many film festivals as possible, because they occur on weekends. I book colleges and universities on weekdays and film festivals and media art centers on weekends. On one tour I booked four consecutive film festivals and averaged three to five college and university bookings each of those four weeks.

IT'S NOT ALWAYS A PARTY

I have a great appreciation for all the work it takes to put on a film festival. It requires thousands of hours and a real dedication from the organizers and the volunteers. They've been working on this for a full year and by the time the festival rolls around these people want to party. And who can blame them?

When I arrive at a film festival I'm not ready to party, although I have been known to rise to the occasion. I get a lot of shit from festival people, usually the volunteers, that I'm wimping out, I'm too old, I can't keep up.

I tell them that they're only at one film festival each year. I've been at three or four in the last month. If they continue to give me grief I say I'll be right back as I have to take Moses for a walk and I sneak quietly back to my hotel room.

Once again Moses becomes my excuse to get out of something. But I always do walk him.

In addition to screenings, panels, and seminars, film festivals have things going on every night. There are special parties for the VIPs, networking parties, and of course just straight up parties with live music and alcohol.

I attend as many events as possible so I can meet lots of people. If it's an event for sponsors I talk up the festival so they will continue to support it. If it's a party just for filmmakers I want to meet as many as possible because so much of what we do is about networking. And you never know what kind of interesting people you're going to meet or stories you're going to hear.

At these parties I limit my alcohol intake, or try to anyway. I look at these events as work. I'm promoting myself, my workshop, the festival, whatever. The people who run film festivals know each other and they talk. You don't want them talking about what an asshole you were or how you got really drunk and made a fool of yourself throwing up in the corner. For the record, I've never done that.

I always tell filmmakers to look at film festivals as part of their marketing plan. They need to go to as many as they can and be pleasant and respectful to the people who run it. If you're not, the next time they look at one of your films – as much as they may like it – they might pass on it because they don't want to deal with you.

DON'T PISS OFF THE AUDIENCE

I was at a film festival and there were problems with the projection. A lot of the films didn't look good and it was a technical problem. I've been to enough film festivals to know that despite their best intentions sometimes these things happen. The staff is trying to fix it because they know it's making everyone look bad including them. The filmmakers usually get the short end because the audience has no idea if this is how your film really looks. They're seeing it for the first and probably only time and don't care about projection problems they just want to watch the film.

At this festival, most filmmakers just dealt with it. One filmmaker didn't. He got up for his Q&A and immediately said, "I don't know why I went to the trouble to shoot 35mm. It looks like shit here on this lousy projector. I can't believe it. What a waste of time. Alright, are there any questions?"

No one asked a single question. This guy was in a lousy mood and no one wanted to engage him. No matter how good his film was, after that no one's ever going to invite him back and I'm sure once word got out about his attitude it closed a lot of doors for him whether he knows it or not.

As the Buddha says, "Don't be an asshole."

Young filmmakers always ask if I have a film in the festival.

I say, "No. I'm here to teach a seminar," or "I'm one of the judges." These filmmakers can't get away fast enough. It's like I have something hanging from my nose.

They assume I'm not a filmmaker, so I must not be able to help them. Which is incredibly shortsighted on their part. You never know who you're going to meet and who they might know.

There's a dress code at film festivals. Obviously there's lots of black and faded Levi's because everyone's an "artist." (Hey wait a minute, that's what I wear...)

There's also lots of what I call "nerd-wear." Retro plaid shirts that are buttoned up to the top with off-brand jeans. Most people get really dressed up for the parties while others take casual to a new low, although I've never seen anyone wear pajamas to a screening or party, and thank God for that.

The bigger and more well known a festival is, the nicer people dress because it's all about being seen. And oddly enough, the smaller and more out of the way a festival is the more people also dress up. I think that's because the people who go to the smaller festivals look at it as a big deal and they want to look nice. The small festivals are my favorites, the ones people put on and go to because they genuinely love movies.

I've been lucky enough to sit on quite a few panels with people whose work I admire. I'm not a name dropper, but... at one festival, I'm sitting next to Lloyd Kaufman, founder of Troma Entertainment, (*The Toxic Avenger, Surf Nazi's Must Die, Poultrygeist*). The moderator always starts his questions with Lloyd, then me, and then the rest of the panel. Lloyd is hilarious! He's fast on his feet and has the audience in hysterics. Now I like to think I'm an amusing guy, but Lloyd is tearing up the place and the best I can get is a mild chuckle.

Finally on question four, I leap to my feet and yell at the moderator, "Stop starting with Lloyd! He's killing me. Start at another part of the panel and please don't make me have to follow Lloyd again."

The audience is shocked by my outburst. You could hear a pin drop in the room if anyone had a pin.

Lloyd calmly taps me on the shoulder and says, "There, there Kelley. It'll be alright…"

And the audience goes crazy.

I love Lloyd and we've done panels together since, but I never sit next to him and I always feel sorry for the poor bastard who does.

SOME PEOPLE JUST DON'T LIKE ME

My buddy Jim calls and says we should do a panel at this film festival in Austin. I laugh and say I'm happy to be on a panel with him but don't put my name on any submission forms because I'm not liked there. I've written some things on my blog that have been critical of large festivals and apparently a lot of people read my blog so word got back to some of these festivals, like I hoped it would.

I've been told that my name has popped up at various meetings and some of the things said about me are not very nice. But if my writing has caused any of these people to re-think how they run their festival and make it accessible for more filmmakers, then that's fine by me. I have enough friends.

Jim and I decide to propose a panel on dialogue for film called, "How to Avoid Fixing It In The Mix," or something like that.

We put together a proposal, Jim sends it off, and I forget about it.

Jim calls a couple weeks later and says I have to re-write the proposal. "Why do I have to re-write it? We sent it under your name."

As it turns out Jim pitched two proposals and you're only allowed to send in one so he put the second one under my name.

"Are you crazy, now it's never going to get approved."

"It's not a big deal. Let's just re-write this thing."

A few weeks later, I hear from friends that our workshop is listed on the festival website and it's getting a lot of votes. Attendees vote for the panels they want to see and that's one of the criteria that's used on approving them. It's not a big deal because from what I understand the number of votes is not the ultimate decider. I still believe there's no way they're going to let me do a panel.

Jim calls to update me about the votes.

"You know, man, I've been thinking you're full of shit. And since I know a few people there I figured I'd make a phone call, check in, and mention that I'd submitted a panel with you."

"And?"

"So I'm talking to my friend and I say I've known you for years and you're a great guy. I ask if she's ever heard of you? ... There's a long pause and then she finally says that she knows who you are, and that I was the only person she knew who had ever said anything nice about you. What the hell did you do?"

"Nothing. In fact I've never met any of them. I've just written that I think a lot of big festivals aren't about independent filmmaking anymore. It's a tight clique, like one big high school, and unless you're a part of the clique you don't stand a chance of getting much help even if you get in. I actively tell people not to submit to those festivals because they're a joke. But I've never written anything bad about any of the people personally. Who knows, I might like 'em if I ever met 'em!"

"Yeah, well, that's not going to happen. They really don't like you."

Our panel was accepted.

Jim and I met in Berkeley about twenty-five years ago. He heard that I worked with John Callahan, the quadriplegic cartoonist. John was confined to a wheelchair and had a vicious non-PC sense of humor. Jim's also in a wheelchair and loves John's take on disabilities. I have to say that Jim and John are two of the funniest people I know especially when it comes to their disabilities. And they don't give a shit if you're offended by what they say. I'm not. That's why we've been friends for so many years.

Moses and I arrive at the festival. He's tired from all of the travel so he stays at a friend's house while I go to the convention center to pick up my official badge (which is free since I'm doing a panel) and the rest of the swag they give out. The person behind the counter makes a point of telling me the type of badge I have, its worth in dollars, and what events it's good for.

I figure this is probably a good time to meet the organizers so they can see that I'm not Satan. As it turns out (or so I'm told), they rarely come to the convention center. They're usually at the theaters with the special guests.

Wandering around, my first take-away is that there's an awful lot of people but no one's talking. I see people everywhere but they're all looking at their phones or their laptops. I see very little socializing.

At most film festivals, conferences, or other film related events people are making contacts, talking about the business, seeing old friends, all sorts of interaction. Not here. There are some people talking but not on the scale I'm used to. Mostly people are sitting on the floor or leaning against walls and they're glued to their screens.

Wow!

Eventually I find myself at the hospitality suite that's been set aside for panelists and guests. I check in. The volunteer sees my name and suddenly becomes wary.

This is not the first time this has happened. I've received calls from interns and volunteers and they all had a hitch in their voice, like they're afraid to talk to me. Did someone tell them I was an asshole or something?

Every time I talk to the volunteers I'm amazingly polite and thank them profusely for giving me whatever information they're passing on. I can hear the confusion in their voices, which pleases me to no end. And I can imagine later conversations.

"I called that Angry Filmmaker Guy, you know, the one that's supposed to be such an asshole. He seems really nice."

'That Angry Guy was really funny and asked me all sorts of questions about myself."

"Why do people keep saying he's a dick?"

As this volunteer is checking me in and telling me what's going on, I listen politely and ask a couple questions.

At the end, he drops a small bomb.

"And you're not allowed to sell any merchandise at your panel."

"Excuse me?"

"You're not allowed to sell any merchandise at your panel."

"Why not?"

"I don't know. I was just told to tell everyone that."

Not sell merchandise! Who the fuck do they think they are? They're not paying me. I paid my own expenses to get here and I have to pay my expenses while I'm here, and I can't sell any merch? How the fuck do they expect me to make a living?

Now I could have confronted this poor volunteer right then and lit him up like a Christmas tree. But I know he's only passing information down from someone else. I never shoot the messenger.

Now, on one level I can understand them not wanting people

to turn their panels into giant sales pitches. That makes sense to me. But that's not what I do. I do my panel or workshop, then let the audience know that my merchandise is available afterward.

Most places pay me. They give me an honorarium, lodging, meals – they really take care of me. But they know that I also make money off of my books, T-shirts, and DVDs. That's how I'm able to do this.

I'm pissed because the festival is selling all their own stuff and they charge a fortune for their screening passes. Sorry gang, I will not play by your rules if I don't think your rules are fair.

I meet Jim later for a drink and tell him what I learned.

"What are you gonna do?"

"Sell my shit."

"If you do you're probably not gonna get asked back."

"We're probably not going to get asked back. You're linked to me. You okay with that?"

"Sure, what the hell."

The next day Jim and I meet in the VIP lounge and we are very pleasant. A volunteer takes us to our room as the panel before us ends. We're told one more time how we only have a certain amount of time and they'll signal us when we have ten minutes to go and then a five-minute signal so we can wrap up. And no merchandise sales!

It's a decent sized room and it's fairly full. I'm guessing between fifty and sixty people.

Jim and I are on fire. We discuss a few tricks at the beginning that we feel are important and we open it up to questions throughout the rest of our presentation. Some people have really good questions. Some people don't have any kind of question that we can decipher they just want to hear themselves talk. People are laughing and taking notes and I feel like they're learning.

Our panel cruises right along and before I know it we get the ten-minute signal.

"I just noticed that we only have ten minutes left so we're going to need to start wrapping this up. But before we go any further I just wanted to let all of you know that we're not allowed to sell any of our merchandise here. Now I know that some of you are wondering what's up here in my suitcase? It's full of copies of my book for fifteen dollars, which I'm not allowed to sell. And T-shirts also for fifteen dollars and then there are my DVDs that are ten dollars, but I can't sell those either. I'm sure you've all noticed the suitcase is open and I can't stop you from looking through it. I also can't stop you from giving me fifteen dollars for a book or a T-shirt or ten dollars for a DVD. But I want you to know that I am not supposed to sell any of this."

Our audience is laughing. The volunteers aren't. I look at Jim, who just smiles. So I continue.

"Have I ever told you all about my grandmother? Grammy, as we call her. Well Grammy needs an operation really badly, and I'm her sole means of support, but since I can't sell any of my merch, I'm not sure how Grammy is going to survive..."

Suddenly Jim speaks up.

"Hey man, fuck your grandmother! I'm in a wheelchair!"

The entire place erupts.

I sell quite a bit of merchandise and Jim and I get the hell out of there. We decide not to go back to the VIP lounge.

"Think they'll cancel our passes?"

"Can they?"

"Don't know. By the way, nice touch with the wheelchair comment."

"It's all about the timing."

Jim and I split up at that point. He has other things to do and I have a couple panels I want to check out before I hit the road. I leave town the next day. I lost money on this part of my tour, but it's not as bad as it could have been.

I have no idea if there's any reaction from the powers that be to our panel. I'm sure I've provided them with more ammunition to say bad things about me. But hey, I've been there once, I don't need to go back.

And for those of you that are wondering, my grandmother died when I was fourteen.

PARKING LOT CAMPING

It's funny, isn't it? You're trying to sleep but you want light. I want it quiet and yet I also want to sleep in an area that has traffic. Somehow people coming and going in a well-lit parking lot makes you feel safer.

The van is always full, so to get in and out using the side door I have to step over Moses who's always curled up on his bed right next to it. It's quite a stretch but after a while we both get pretty good at me getting in and out. Moses just lies there looking at me, praying that I don't step on him either coming or going. I'm always amazed at how he never moves when I have to step over him. He totally trusts that I'm not going to step on him. And I never have to worry that he's going to make a sudden move and knock me over.

There are nights when I'm exhausted, but no matter how

heavy a sleeper I am, if Moses has any running dreams he wakes me up. You know the kind: He starts whining or even barking and his legs are moving like he's running in place and yet he's sound asleep. There were a few times early on when he'd scare the hell out of me with one of his sound asleep barks.

And the snoring. Listening to a one-hundred-and-twenty-pound dog snore in close quarters is quite the treat. There are some nights I wonder if I'll ever get any sleep.

I always look for a truck stop to spend the night in but sometimes I'm too tired and the next one is too far away. So I go for the next best thing.

Walmart doesn't mind people spending the night as long as you're respectful of the property and they figure you'll come in and buy things. A buddy of mine was asked to leave when he and his wife and brother pitched a tent. I guess that went a little too far.

I'm not a fan of Walmart because they don't pay most of their employees a living wage. The fact that they have trained some managers to teach employees how to get benefits from the federal government is beyond horrible. The family that owns Walmart is among the richest in this country and their employees are underpaid. That's deplorable.

Their bathrooms, though, are usually clean.

The first few times I wandered into the store with my toothbrush and toothpaste some employees were not amused. It's also the same when I walk in carrying a towel and soap. They know I'm here to use their facilities for free and I'm not going to buy anything. But they never say anything to me directly.

Now I use bottled water from my cooler to brush my teeth and clean up out in the parking lot. I keep all my empty water bottles in a bag in the back of the van and refill them whenever I find a decent source, which is often a drinking fountain at Walmart. I'm sure this doesn't endear me to their employees either, but on the road you gotta do what you gotta do.

Wandering the aisles at three a.m. when I can't sleep is always interesting. I'm fascinated by the employees who work the night shift and the people who shop at that time, too. Three a.m. in a Walmart gives you an interesting take on America.

There aren't many old or young people shopping then. Mostly it's families buying groceries and necessities. It's not just Mom and Dad. It's the kids, too. The parent's look like they just got off work and the kids look wide-awake. It makes me wonder how these kids will feel when they have to get up and go to school. They aren't just browsing, checking out toys, or electronics, or anything like that. They're sticking to the food aisles. The kids are all well behaved and they're working together to finish up as soon as possible.

From what I can tell they're working people who are just trying to get by. I wonder how many of these folks are working multiple jobs. They usually pay for everything with a mix of cash and credit/debit cards. I rarely see EBT cards. It's tired people paying their own way and buying a lot of rice and beans and bread. I also hear a lot of laughter among these families, which is something I rarely hear in any grocery store.

The parking lot is where the extremes come together. There are really expensive motor homes and trailers. I rarely see other vans like mine, and only occasionally a car with people sleeping in it. The vehicles that are driven by the people who camp here are totally different than the vehicles of those who shop here. Most of the shoppers cars are at least ten years old and look and sound pretty rough. There are more pick-ups than cars and the cars are mostly American made.

The motor homes are mostly pretty new and they're very well kept. Most of my fellow campers are retired. Some of them live in their motor homes full-time, others are on vacation. They get tired, see a Walmart and pull in. They camp at Walmart because they're convenient, safe, and free, and when you're retired you need to stretch every dollar. A lot of these folks don't buy food at Walmart. They talk about issues of quality and price and many of them don't feel that Walmart has the best prices on food. I walk down the aisles one night looking at food prices and I have to agree. When you look at the weight and the price it doesn't add up to savings. And yet they sell themselves as having the lowest prices. Interesting.

LAND OF ENCHANTMENT

Spending the night in the parking lot in Los Cruces, New Mexico, is an interesting experience. What makes it interesting is that I'm the minority. As I walk through the store killing time before I go to sleep I find that almost everyone I encounter (employees and patrons) are either Native American or Hispanic.

That's not to say that I've never been in the minority when I travel. I stay in different ethnic areas all over the country, but never in a predominantly Native American area. I've driven through reservations in other states but if I stop it's usually just for gas. There's not much interaction.

Here, I'm the one who stands out. I'm not worried, scared, or anything like that. Everyone I encounter is friendly and I get comments on my Oregon license plates. But to be in this kind of environment is a real change for a white guy. I think it's important that everyone at some point experiences what it's like to be a minority in their own country. Maybe it'll help us better understand each other.

I love New Mexico. It's one of the most beautiful places I've ever been. The terrain is unique and the views are impressive. Anyone who has ever driven through New Mexico will tell you that you know when you enter the state because the terrain is so different from the states that surround it. The rock formations, the mesas, everything feels like you're in another land.

I have a friend who used to live right outside of Santa Fe and when I'd stay with him the place seemed unreal. Sitting on his patio at night the sky went on forever. It was incredibly dark out where he lived and the sky was filled with stars. It was an overwhelming site. It makes you feel tiny.

There's so much money in Santa Fe, so many white people and so many "haves." There's also intense poverty when you get outside of town and that's where I didn't see many white people. It's a huge divide.

Some people think New Mexico is desolate and I couldn't disagree more. It feels like it hasn't been tamed the way so many other places have. The terrain is rugged as are the people who live there.

New Mexico seems very romantic in a really wild and rugged way – it puts a spell over me. I always look forward to going back there.

THAT CAN'T BE ITS REAL NAME

On the other hand there's this place in the middle of nowhere, Effingham, Illinois. Well that's not entirely true. It's near the intersection of two interstates (57 and 70) so I guess that's somewhere.

In the last seven years this place has grown from a dot in the road with just a few amenities to a boomtown that's all about strip malls, fast food chains, and cheap motel chains. I'm sure there's a real town there somewhere but all I ever see when I pull off the Interstate are the strip malls.

I'm traveling through the area and I hear on the radio that a huge storm is coming. And yes, I do listen to the radio when I travel. How else would I know what's going on weather wise?

And why is it, whenever I'm on the road all I ever hear on NPR is fundraising? But I'll save that rant for another time.

The thought of sleeping in a parking lot during a major storm isn't sounding fun. I've done it before. I don't like being rocked to sleep by the wind as the rain is lashing all sides of the van. I splurge for a motel room for Moses and me, a Motel 6 right next to Walmart. It turns out to be quite a storm. In our room I hear the rain and wind all night. I'm not sure if Moses heard any of it. Judging by his snoring, probably not.

Moses gets me up early so we can go out and check for new smells. I'm wondering if there's any major damage. As we walk through the Walmart parking lot I'm amazed at the number of vehicles that are here. There must be fifty semi-trucks and at least fifty motor homes and trailers. I guess no one wanted to drive through that storm.

One night in Georgia, I'm too tired to drive any further and there's a Walmart. I pull in next to a small motor home and take Moses for a nice long walk. The weather's warm and as far as he's concerned there are a lot of places to mark. I'm just happy to be out of the van.

When walking a big dog you are always on alert for dead things or food. For whatever reason Moses likes to roll in dead things and even though he's fed regularly he can't resist any food that's been left on the ground. And you never know what kind of food he might come across. So wherever we walk I'm ever vigilant. I used to worry about squirrels because he would lunge at them and when a hundred-and-twenty-pound dog lunges, you feel it in your shoulder. As he gets older he appears to have adopted a "live and let live" attitude as far as squirrels go which is much easier on my shoulder.

As we walk back to the van I see a security guy talking to the owner of the small motor home. I walk up.

"Is there a problem here?"

"Is that your van?"

"Yeah."

"I was just saying to this fellow here that I'd appreciate it if you fellows would move your cars over to where those other campers are. It'll be easier for me to keep my eye on you tonight. It's safer if you're all parked together."

I'm not sure exactly what he means by "safer if you're all parked together," but he says it in a friendly way. "Safer" is really important to me since I have tinted windows in the van but no curtains. Light does come in but I don't think you can really see inside. Besides, my sleeping platform is just below the window line so I usually feel safe.

THERE ARE 42 PLACES NAMED OXFORD AND I'M STUCK IN THIS ONE

One late night outside of Oxford, Ohio, heavy fog is rolling in and it's been a long day of driving. It's time to call it a night. I find a Walmart, take Moses for his evening walk, then crawl into my sleeping bag for the night.

I am jolted awake at three a.m. to a semi pulling in.

One thing I hate – I understand it but I hate it just the same – is when you're settled in for the night and a semi pulls in and idles all night long. I can't sleep. At all. It's horrible.

Now I understand that sometimes they can't turn off their trucks for different reasons, but could they at least park farther away from the rest of us? Twice I've had to move my van in the middle of the night because a semi was keeping me awake. And this is one of those nights.

I climb out of my warm sleeping bag and crawl between the front seats trying unsuccessfully not to step on anything. I start the van and move to another part of the parking lot. I crawl back through the seats and into the warm sleeping bag and I'm out.
I wake up at first light, around six a.m. It's even foggier, if that's possible. I roll over and go back to sleep. Seven o'clock, still really thick.

Finally at seven-thirty I get up and take Moses out. Visibility is maybe thirty feet. We have breakfast in the van. At eight-thirty I decide I can't wait any longer. We pull on to the interstate and I drop into a line of cars that are all moving at a pretty good clip.

I hate driving in the fog so I try to find a semi or a group of cars and hang with them hoping that if one of them gets into a wreck I'll have enough time to slow down, swerve, do whatever to avoid it. I know from news reports of chain reaction accidents in fog that this is unlikely, but I continue to fool myself anyway. And unlike Steinbeck's travels, I have deadlines. My schedule is tight enough that there is always a school, media art center, or film festival that I need to get to so I can speak.

I like to think that whoever is leading the pack knows what they're doing, where they're going or can see better than I can. I recall a conversation with a friend of mine, who said, "The lead car is probably some teenager with a latte in one hand, talking on their cell phone to their boyfriend or girlfriend, and can't see any better than anyone else. They're just driving to work not thinking about the fog."

This thought hits me square in the face. Shit. We're all lemmings running toward the cliff.

At this moment I feel like I have no choice but to keep driving and hope my buddy is wrong. I hope that God loves fools and will protect us from ourselves. They say there are no atheists in foxholes. I also believe that when I'm driving in thick fog.

It's a good hour before I finally come up over a hill and the fog is gone. I've lived to drive another day.

Now I don't want to suggest that Walmart is the only place to sleep when you're on the road. I sleep in truck stops, rest stops, and I've done stealth camping.

Truck stops are great because they're well lit and people don't bother you, at least they've never bothered me. Since they're open twenty-four hours a day you can always go inside to use the bathroom, get coffee, or whatever. The downside can be the noise from the semis, but when you park on the car side of the truck stop, it's usually pretty quiet.

With rest areas it depends on the area. They aren't lit as well but that might be because they're smaller and in isolated areas so the light drop-off outside of the rest area makes it feel so much darker. Being right off the freeway they're usually noisy and I've encountered some pretty strange people.

One morning in a rest area in Ohio, I came upon a shirtless, heavily tattooed rockabilly guy who was missing a few teeth. He was pacing back and forth next to an old '55 Chevy brushing his teeth and spitting in the parking lot. Hanging out the window was a pit bull wearing a spiked collar with real spikes. On the side of the car was a painting of the devil with a phrase about hell. It was not a religious phrase. He was advocating a rather wild life style and fuck anyone who had a problem with it and him. I can't remember exactly what it said and he was in no mood to let anyone take a photo.

He was talking loudly to no one, and taking great pleasure in scaring the hell out of everyone. This guy was crazy looking, even by my standards. One distinguished looking older gentleman from a huge RV walked over to speak with him. He glared at the old man and said something (I couldn't hear). The old man turned around and walked straight back to his RV.

Moses took no notice of this guy and his dog. He marked some turf and then we drove off towards our next adventure.

One night in Pennsylvania there were six cars parked in a rest area all with people sleeping in them. The cars were loaded with family possessions. It reminded me of a modern scene from

The Grapes of Wrath. It appeared to be a group of families migrating somewhere.

A rest area at night always makes me feel vulnerable. Sure, they're patrolled by state police, but not very often. At night they feel really isolated. Some of them feel that way during the day, too. They feel very transient and if something does happen people can just slip back out on to the highway and be gone. Most of the time I don't feel comfortable sleeping there. Even with a big dog.

Stealth camping can be dicey. I prefer to do it in a city that I've been to before and I have a feel for the area. You don't want to camp in a bad neighborhood, but you also don't want to be in such a good neighborhood that people call the cops because there's a strange van with out-of-state plates in front of their house.

A city park is good, but neighborhoods are best because you're least likely to be bothered. If I'm stealth camping I set up the back of the van in advance. I inflate the air mattress, unroll the sleeping bag, take Moses for a walk, brush my teeth, all of those things I need to do before I crash. Then I find a quiet place to park and climb between the front seats to the back. I make as little noise as possible.

I always set my alarm for just before it gets light so that I can be out of there before people get up. Then I find a gas station, restaurant or wherever to get coffee, walk Moses and clean myself up before we head back out on the road.

TRAVELING with a DOG

Driving through Missouri and the rain's been coming down in buckets all day. After a hellish two-hundred-mile drive and a poor turnout at my screening, I just want to sleep and get the hell outta town in the morning. I'm tired and cold.

I check into this cheap motel by the freeway. This place has seen better days as have the people hanging around the lobby. The paint is peeling and the lighting makes an already depressing place feel suicidal. The patrons are all pretty sketchy. It feels more halfway house than motel. I could leave, but my only other choice this night would be to sleep in the van. No thanks.

I grab the important stuff from the van: laptop, camera, a few clothes, and the dog. Everything else is expendable if the van's broken into. Please don't let it be broken into.

Moses has two leashes. A six-footer and a three-footer. I keep the short leash in the van as a back up in case I lose the regular leash or it breaks. I'm tired and accidentally grab the short leash.

As we move across the dingy lobby people are staring at this huge dog on a very short leash. I have it wrapped it around my hand so it's less than two feet in length. Moses is right next to me.

As I reach out to press the filthy button on the elevator, the door opens and three seedy looking characters stand there. Years of hard living and hard partying have taken a toll on their faces. These guys are just plain ugly. My guess is they've seen the insides of more than a few jail cells.

These guys glare at me as the doors slowly open.

Fuck! I just want to go to my room and sleep. I don't want any hassles.

They're sizing me up for something. Then they see Moses on the short leash. These guys can't get away from us fast enough. They're obviously afraid of the dog.

I look down at Mo, hoping his tail isn't wagging. He's just staring at these guys as they pass. He doesn't growl or bark but the fur on his back is up. These guys see this. One of them says, "Excuse me, sir," as he passes by.

I give Mo an extra snack when we get to the room. There are times when he's a big sweet goof ball but I know that if anyone tries to mess with either of us his demeanor will change in a second. At least I hope so.

Traveling with a dog brings a whole different dynamic to the road.

ALWAYS CARRY PLASTIC BAGS

All dogs mark where they've been and Moses is no exception. I'm not sure why he feels the urge to do this, as he'll probably never be back to some of these places. And if we do go back, it's months or years later. I know dogs have an extraordinary sense of smell but I can't see him recognizing his own scent after that long.

He also doesn't care where he relieves himself, which is why I always carry bags. Moses has no shame or sense of embarrassment. He's gone in front of groups of Japanese tourists, around cops or other symbols of authority, and elderly people. A good crowd is like a laxative for Moses. Then, like the little man on the scooter who follows the horses in a parade, I clean up the evidence so that we'll be invited back.

When it comes to lodging, a lot of places will let you bring a small dog in. Hell, if your dog is small enough, you can sneak it in and I have friends who do that.

If you have a big dog, the rules are different. Moses looks like a small brown bear when he gets out of the van. There's no way I can ever sneak him in anywhere.

Actually, that's not true. When Fiona and I were on tour one summer we went to the UFVA Conference in Denton, Texas. We stayed in the dorms on the university campus and dogs are apparently not allowed in the dorms. It was way too hot to leave him in the van and we were lucky enough to be given a room at the far end of the hall, near an exit door. For three days Fiona and I snuck him in and out of the room and, although my friends knew he was in there, I never heard anything from the powers that be.

I was given a copy of the AAA Guide to Pet Friendly Hotels and Motels across the country, (thank you, Debby). Sometimes it works and sometimes it doesn't. Some places say they no longer take pets, some deny they ever took pets, and some blame the current pet policy on a new owner.

HOTEL/MOTEL ETIQUETTE

I don't take Moses with me when I check in. I prefer to pay for the room before they get to see him. I tell the desk clerk that I have a mature and very mellow dog and I won't leave him in the room by himself.

Moses has a way of making himself comfortable in any situation. When he walks into a new room the first thing he does, after a quick reconnaissance (and no, he doesn't mark the room), is to pick which bed he's going to sleep on. Which is okay if there are two beds, but if there aren't he climbs up on the one bed and dares me to move him.

If I'm still unloading I let him be, which only makes it harder to move him later.

One of the worst things I ever did was allow Moses to sleep on the bed. I have a king-sized bed at home so it isn't a problem.

There's more than enough room for both of us.

On the road, when the bed is a double, or on those rare occasions a twin, it's a problem. Moses is so used to sleeping on a bed that he's going to get up there no matter how many times I throw him off. He just waits for me to fall asleep, then tries to climb up quietly. He does nothing quietly.

My next dog will not be allowed on the bed. Lesson learned.

THE GOOD

At the D.C. Shorts Film Festival, Jon always puts us up in a pet-friendly hotel.

The first hotel we stayed at in D.C. ruined Moses forever. The Hotel Monaco is part of a small chain of boutique hotels across the country, and it's very fancy. Apparently the owner is a dog person so dogs are always welcome. Even big dogs.

Checking in, the staff takes an immediate liking to Moses and gives him treats, thus insuring his undying loyalty. They know I'm going to be at the festival and so with my permission they go to the room and take him out for walks. Yes, they don't mind if I leave him in the room during the day – they even give me a tag to put on the doorknob to let the cleaning people know he's in the room.

In the evenings they bring him to the lobby where he stays behind the front desk. When I return they say, "Moses is back here." He'll be all stretched out, snoring.

I tell them they can let kids pet him because when kids see him they go crazy. By the end of our stay they're sorry to see Moses go.

A week later a note arrives at my house with a thank-you card from the staff and pictures of Moses hanging out with the employees. He had more fun than I did.

THE BAD

A couple days later I pull into a motel in North Carolina that the university has set up for me. At the front desk I inform them I have my dog with me.

"We don't allow dogs."

"I'm staying here as a guest of the university. I've been assured that everything was taken care of as far as the dog and myself." I'm friendly, but firm. The manager insists they knew nothing about the dog.

After a brief stand off the manager says the dog can stay but I will have to give them a one-hundred-and-fifty-dollar deposit that's fully refundable if the dog doesn't damage the room.

I'm happy to do that but I want to do it in cash and when I check out in the morning I want a representative to check the room and I want my deposit returned at that time as there will be no damage to the room.

They aren't happy, but they agree to it. They give me a room near a back exit and ask if I would come and go by the side door so their other guests wouldn't see Moses. I'm fine with that.

The professor I worked with for this gig is shocked when I relay this information to her as she'd told them about the dog and was assured everything was taken care of.

The first thing Moses does is jump on the bed, which has a beautiful white bedspread and he's in one of his major shedding periods. Who am I kidding? Labs shed 24/7 year-round.

The next morning I go to the front desk and ask to have the room checked so I can get my deposit back. Everyone's busy and they can't do it right then. I ask for my deposit back because I need to hit the road. They can't do that until the room is checked. I assure them there's no damage to the room and to please return my deposit per our agreement. I'm getting annoyed.

Suddenly they find someone on staff who can do it. The report comes back that the room is fine although there's short brown hair all over the bedspread. The desk clerk looks like she's not sure whether she should charge me or not.

"I'm sure a fine hotel like this washes the sheets and bed spread after each guest leaves, don't you?" I say politely.

She looks flustered, then reaches into the till and hands me my deposit back.

THE UGLY

There are times when out of necessity I stay at some less than stellar places and that's when I'm happy to have Moses with me.

He rarely barks but when he does the windows shake and he means business.

Moses is in charge of security. I play this one venue in Baltimore and it's not a bad neighborhood, let's say it's "in transition." I usually park in front of the place and invariably there are a couple of rough looking locals hanging around.

I always let Moses out when I first get there. We walk up and down the street so he can look around and mark his turf before he gets back in the van.

In all of the times I've played here, I've seen a lot of broken glass on the street but I've never had any problems. I also never leave Moses in the van over night. I bring him inside when it gets dark, but they don't know that.

MOSES KNOWS MORE THAN I DO

One night I'm doing a show at a different venue, a place I've never been before. A couple friends say it's a worse neighborhood than the one I stay in but I should be okay.

I use MapQuest to get there. Which is easy because it's still light out. I neglect to print out reverse directions. I'll just do it in my head, no problem.

Driving back after midnight of course I make a wrong turn. Not that I know I've made a wrong turn because I have no idea which turn is wrong, but suddenly I'm in an area I don't recognize.

The streets are empty as I look for a place to turn around.

I see cameras on telephone polls. Being a rube from Oregon I think, "Hey, they've got red light cameras to ticket people who run stop lights just like we do. With so little traffic I'm sure they don't make a lot of money off those cameras."

I'm still looking for a place to turn around when I see a giant motor home with the Baltimore Police insignia on the side. I wonder what that's doing here?

There's no activity and I can't tell if anyone is in it or not. This part of Baltimore doesn't seem to be very well lit, or is it just my imagination?

I turn around in an empty parking lot and head back the way I came. I think. This doesn't look familiar either. I hang a U-turn. Where am I? None of this looks familiar.

I'm lost. I'm also feeling funny about this area. I see a few small groups of people on the streets, mostly male, just hangin' out.

I notice Moses, who has been sitting up looking out the window and is now laying flat on the floor absolutely silent, and he's wide a wake. What's up with that?

I pass by the police motor home four more times but still can't find my way out of this area. Is that someone looking out the curtain?

I'm turning around in parking lots, making U-turns, slowing down and looking at street signs. I'm so turned around and confused. I might not ever get back to where I'm staying. People on the street are staring at me as I drive by. Have I passed these people before? Maybe I should ask one of them for directions? Maybe not.

I drive around for an hour. Okay maybe ten minutes. I finally see a familiar looking street so I hang a right. I go a few blocks and see another street that I know so I hang a left. Soon I'm on familiar streets, heading back to where we're staying.

I notice Moses is sitting back up looking out the window.

We finally arrive back where we're staying. Getting out of the van I'm immediately approached by a disheveled looking pothead.

"Hey man, I just ran outta gas and I'm tryin' to get home. Can you loan me twenty dollars so I can put gas in my car?"

I love the concept of *loaning* this guy I've never seen before twenty dollars. How does he expect to pay me back?

"You got a gas can?"

"Uh no."

"What kind a car you driving?"

He pauses. "A Chevy?"

"Just a Chevy."

He nods slowly.

I hand him two bucks from my pocket.

"It's all I got."

He looks disappointed. He turns to leave as I let Moses out of the van.

"You know you're not fooling anyone with that story. Next time, get a gas can," I say.

The next morning I meet a friend for breakfast and mention my discovery of Baltimore's red-light cameras.

"What are you talking about?"

I told her what I'd seen the night before.

"Where were you?"

"I don't know. Coming back from my show I got lost."

I told her where I'd been coming from.

"You have no idea where you were."

"No. I was lost."

"No. You have no idea *where* you were. Those cameras on the poles aren't for people running red lights. They're to keep track of gang activity."

"Really?"

"They weren't aimed at the intersections, were they?"

"Now that you mention it..."

"That motor home was probably full of cops, and here you are making U-turns and cutting through parking lots? A white guy ... in a van ... with out-of-state plates. Even I won't go into that area at night and I'm not white!"

"That bad?"

"That bad."

"I guess the Baltimore PD has a ton of footage of me."

"I'm surprised they didn't stop you."

I guess God does protect fools. But in case he doesn't, I got a GPS unit.

THE MYTH of SEX on the ROAD

The road can get very lonely. Sometimes you want a little comfort.

I'm walking with William Akers across the Vanderbilt campus on a beautiful spring day. The weather's warm and everyone's out. Women in sundresses, or shorts and T-shirts, guys in shorts, and tank tops. All worshiping the sun.

As we walk, William says in his matter-of-fact way, "You realize that to all of these young women, we're invisible. The only time they ever want to have anything to do with me is when they come to my office because they want a grade change."

As a kid I wanted to be invisible, that was my favorite superpower. Apparently I had to wait until I got older.

When guys hear that I tour cross-country showing my films, I'm always met with the same questions. "What's it like hanging out with all those college girls? Are they wild? Do you have a lot of sex?"

Apparently a lot of guys and a few ex-girlfriends think I'm having copious amounts of sex out on the road. Actually the ex-girlfriends were a bit more accusatory.

I hate to disappoint any of you but – "No!"

As an old friend of mine used to say, "No one comes to Hollywood to fuck a sound editor." I would modify that a bit and say, "No one comes to any of my workshops and screenings to fuck a fifty-something-year-old independent filmmaker." But maybe that's just me.

I'm of an age where I have a pretty good idea who and what I am. If I ever tried to hit on any of those college girls they would probably run screaming from me yelling, "Ohhhh, that old man hit on me." Or "He's old enough to be my grandfather. Ick!"

This of course would not do a lot for what's left of my fragile ego.

I'm sure wild parties and mindless sex on the road happened years ago and I missed it. Or maybe a middle-age filmmaker is not as appealing as Mick Jagger or Bono. I don't know. What I can tell you is that I have never been involved in, or seen any, wild sex on the road. Unfortunately.

I apologize for bursting any balloons.

THIS IS A BUSINESS
(THE 70 MPH INTERVIEW)

Unlike Kerouac and Steinbeck, the only way I can manage to drive cross-country is to treat it like a business. I'm promoting my films and books because I have to make a living. There are times when I have newspaper and radio interviews scheduled and I'm not always in the most convenient places to do them.

Sure, it's dangerous, but there are times when I have to do interviews while driving. I have a schedule to keep. In my experience the two best places to do road interviews are Texas and Nebraska because the highways are flat and straight. I can do seventy-plus and keep the conversation going.

The first question is always my favorite.

"Where are you right now?"

"Interstate 80."

"At a rest area?"

"No. Doing seventy-five, heading east. Not sure where exactly, but I need to be in Kansas City by tonight."

"Should I call back at a better time?"

"This is a perfect time. There's hardly any traffic and I'm just listening to music. If I lose you blame it on AT&T."

And the interview proceeds. Which is nice because an interesting interview always breaks up the monotony.

One day I have to do an interview for a newspaper in Tulsa at a specific time and I'm in Ohio. My cell isn't getting any coverage (which is one of the reasons I'm no longer with AT&T) so I pull off the highway. There's an old gas station with a little store attached to it. And right out front is a pay phone. A real pay phone.

Digging through my wallet I find an old phone card that I've saved for just such an occasion. I dial my MCI number and code (fuck, this was a long time ago!) and soon I'm talking to the reporter.

People are coming and going at this small store. Why do they keep staring at me? Moses is lying regally on the ground in front of me watching them. No use keeping him in the van. I'm trying to be as entertaining as possible. Even though I'm on the phone I'm talking with my hands, making faces and laughing. The people going in and out must think I'm a crazy person. This is one of the few times on the road that people don't come up and ask if they can pet Moses. I think they're afraid.

One day I'm in a small diner having a late lunch and doing an interview by phone. The place is pretty empty and I'm trying to keep my voice down so as not to bother the few other customers. I tell the interviewer I'm in Missouri.

Suddenly one of the patrons corrects me quite loudly. "You're in Kansas!"

"Apparently I'm in Kansas." I say to my interviewer.

The guy is glaring at me. My guess is he's not a fan of Missouri.

KEEPING ME HONEST

College newspapers are always the best. I've been asked some great questions that have caught me totally off-guard.

"What's in your left front pants pocket right now?"

"My house key, thirty-seven cents in change, a bottle opener and a guitar pick. And I don't play guitar. Someone gave that to me yesterday. Oh and a screw from the platform in the van. It came undone yesterday and I need to fix it."

"What film do you wish you would have made?"

"Present or past?"

"Past."

"Touch of Evil."

"Why?"

"So I could have cast a real Hispanic for the Charlton Heston role."

And some really strange questions.

"You studied film at USC. How do you think their football team is going to do this year?"

"I never saw the football team play when I was in school. I have no idea how they're going to do any year."

Then there are the questions you get asked when you know that the reporter has not only not seen your work, but they haven't even looked at the bio you sent.

"So *Birddog*, is this a documentary?"

"No, it's a dramatic feature."

"What's it like living in Hollywood?"

"I don't know, I live in Portland."

"What did you think of the last *Star Wars* film?"

"What's this got to do with my screening?"

"I don't know, I was just wondering…"

"I haven't seen it."

"Well, you should."

"Okay. I'll do that."

"It's really good."

"Can we talk about my work?"

"I haven't had a chance to look at the DVD you sent me. Can you tell me about it?"

"It's nothing like *Star Wars*."

Then there's the problem of people telling me they want me to do a screening or a workshop and then canceling just a day or two before I get there. Like it's no big deal.

I had one asshole that suddenly stopped returning my phone calls and emails a week before I was scheduled to show up. It was radio silence.

Finally I leave a message saying, "What's going on? You've booked this and now I don't even know where I'm supposed to be. Is there a hotel or am I staying with someone? You need to get hold of me and let me know what's going on."

I got an email from the guy. "It's not going to work out this time, but maybe on your next tour…"

"Fuck you! There will be no next time and I'm letting my friends in the business know that you are an unreliable piece of shit!"

Of course I didn't write that, although I should have. I just kept repeating it to myself over and over the next few days.

GREEN DAY PLAYED A LOT OF BASEMENTS

There is this urban myth, an industry legend, that I've heard many times in many different places about this "local" kid who booked a show with Green Day before they were famous. The show did well but Green Day had no bookings for the next few days and were so broke that they stayed at the kids house for three days and did shows in his basement every night for whoever was around. For the amount of times and places I've heard this story repeated, Green Day must have played in basements all over the country.

I keep hoping that some rumor or wild myth like that would grow up around one of my tours. If I ever do stay at one person's place for three days I won't be doing shows every night, I'll just be taking advantage of their hospitality.

Sometimes last-minute gigs do work out. My first few years on the road I was much more negotiable than I am now. I used to do a lot of lectures and workshops for free if I didn't have a paying gig. I always felt it was better to be talking to a group of filmmakers or film students for free and try to make merchandise sales than it was to just sit on my ass in a motel room doing nothing. I met a lot of good people that way and made some great friends.

The downside of course is once you do a freebie for someone then they don't want to pay you next time. "Hey man, you did the last one for free."

"Yeah, because I was building my following and I didn't have any other bookings. And last time you had a lot of people show up. We both know I can do it again."

"Well I don't know…maybe next time."

And that would be it.

It's one thing if you aren't sure if I'm any good. Maybe I'm a boring speaker? But these people know I'm good. They just don't believe they should have to pay artists to come speak and that pisses me off.

One guy booked me for a gig at a bookstore where he worked. He's all gung ho and telling me he can get me a really good crowd for a workshop. There's a ton of interest in the area and he knows all sorts of people. He lived in this cool house with a bunch of roommates and was more than happy to put Moses and I up.

It turns out this guy wanted to book me so he could ask me a bunch of questions about his own film. Five people showed up for the workshop and he spent most of the time asking specific questions about fixing problems in his film.

And putting Moses and I up?

He actually just rents a room in this house with a bunch of other people he doesn't know very well. There were no spare rooms so I slept on an air mattress on the floor in the living room, with people coming and going all night. It was obvious he didn't let anyone know I was going to be sleeping there because they looked surprised when they saw me in the morning.

"And by the way, your dog can't stay in the house. He'll have to stay in your car."

"You said that wouldn't be a problem."

"I didn't realize the house has a no-dogs rule."

Basically the guy's an asshole. He knew what he was doing.

My one night there he took me to dinner at the greasiest Vietnamese restaurant I've ever been to. I got back at him, though. The next day I really stunk up the communal bathroom. Not that I felt all that great anyway.

I'M GETTING TOO OLD FOR THIS

In Memphis I stayed at what could best be described as a "crash pad." It was free and my host let me sleep in his bedroom while he slept on the couch. There was one bathroom on the main floor and I think the last time it had been cleaned was in the nineteen-sixties. I thought about keeping my shoes on while I was in the shower. And the shower not only had no water pressure but things appeared to be living on the curtain.

Did I mention it was close to the airport? In fact it was right on the landing path. All night long planes were coming and going every three-to-five minutes, right above my head. Did you know that Memphis is the major hub for Federal Express? I got no sleep.

Luckily the roommates were really nice and I had a great turnout at my screening and workshop so I did all right. At my next stop I went to my hotel room first and showered before my screening. Just in case something decided to hitch a ride on me from that house.

WHEN I FIGHT AUTHORITY... AGAIN

"Can you tell me what happened in Idaho?"
"Excuse me?"
"What happened in Idaho?
"I don't know what you're talking about."

I'm standing at a counter in an immigration office located between the U.S. and Canada. I'm being interrogated by a U.S. immigration officer as I'm coming home from a visit in Canada. I saw some friends and did a workshop at Capilano University. This guy is a major dick.

"Sure you do."
"No seriously, I don't."

Major Dick stares at me. I break first.

"Listen I've driven through Idaho a lot but I've never even been pulled over. I have no idea what you're talking about."

"I need your keys, your wallet and your cell phone. We need to search your van."

"Search the van?"

"Give me your keys, please."

Years ago I was denied entry into Canada. I was doing a job for Freightliner Corporation filming a semi-truck and they wanted me to film it on Victoria Island, as it was a truck specifically designed for Canadian highways. I told the people who hired me that my crew and I would need work permits to shoot in Canada and customs brokers to get the truck and our equipment in and out of the country without a problem. I was assured it would be taken care of.

It wasn't.

A long story short, the customs brokers were there for the truck and the equipment but no work permits were ever obtained and my cinematographer and I were detained at the border, our passports taken, and we were put on the next ferry back to the US. No filming.

The Canadian immigration officer filed a report and now I have a record. Every time I travel internationally I get stopped by immigration authorities. The officials at most of the countries I visit are great. When my name pops up on their computers I explain what happened and how the fuck-up was the fault of my employers. I assure them that I'm not going to be working in their country and I'm free to go.

Coming back into the U.S., however, different story.

It's early morning when I pull up to the border stop. There are hardly any cars here.

I think, "Fantastic, no line, I'll breeze right through."

Followed by, "Shit, these guys have nothing to do. I'm fucked!"

Sure enough.

"Where you coming from?"

"Vancouver."

He takes my passport and looks at his computer. "Would you mind pulling over there?"

That's not really a question, is it? I pull over and an Immigration Guy comes out. This guy is not as intimidating as the southern border patrol guys, but he has kind of a "Dick Swagger" that they must teach these guys in fed school. I have a bad feeling about this.

Which is how I end up inside with him asking about "Idaho." I'm sitting on a bench waiting while he and another agent are searching my van. This shouldn't take too long because there's hardly anything in it.

Finally he comes back and motions me to the counter. Another agent with his arms folded across his chest stands next to him.

"Where's your dog?"

"My dog?"

Major Dick just stares at me.

"He's at home. My friends have cats."

I certainly didn't realize that I'd have to justify leaving Moses at home to immigration. I guess I should have taken his travel bed out of the van before I left.

"Did you know those T-shirts you have are made in Nicaragua?"

"Excuse me?"

"They're imported so you need to pay a duty on them."

"But I didn't buy them outside the US. I bought them in Portland, Oregon, and then had them silk-screened with my logo."

"They're from Nicaragua and you're illegally importing them."

"No, I'm not. I bought them in the U.S. They've been in the van since my last tour ended about a month ago."

"You need to pay the duty."

Okay, wait a minute – I buy T-shirts from a U.S. company, have them silk-screened by a local U.S. company and I have to pay duty on them? WTF? But one look at Major Dick here and I know he has nothing better to do than to hassle me. And he has all day.

"How much is the duty?"

He has this smug look on his face as he looks at his computer and makes a couple calculations.

"Fourteen dollars!"

"Fourteen dollars?"

"Yes. Fourteen dollars!"

Major Dick is really stretching here but better to pay fourteen fucking dollars and get the hell out of here.

I hand him fifteen dollars. I'm tempted to say, "Keep the change, my good man." But decide against it.

He hands me back my keys, wallet, passport and cell phone and a dollar.

"You're free to go."

"Before I go I need some clarification. What's the deal with Idaho? I travel a lot and if something happened there I need to find out so I can clear it up."

He looks at me and says something under his breath.

"Excuse me? I couldn't hear what you said. If there's a problem on my record I wanna take care of it."

He says something again and I still can't hear him.

"My hearing isn't very good, could you speak up?"

"It wasn't Idaho. It said, 'ID.' I just misread the screen."

"ID? So there's nothing about Idaho? I don't have anything on my record about Idaho?"

I see the other agent looking at him and he breaks into a smile for just a moment.

"No sir. There is no problem in Idaho."

"So you misread what it said on the screen and everything on my record is okay?"

Major Dick is not making eye contact with me.

"Yes sir."

"I just want to make sure. Because if there is something on my record that I don't know about I wanna get it all straightened out."

"It's fine."

At this moment I really want to tell this asshole to fuck off! I don't do it because I'm a nice guy, the forgiving sort. And really, I just want to get the hell out of here.

"Thanks, man. You have a great day." I'm surprised I'm able to say this without a hint of sarcasm.

As I turn to leave I look at the other agent. He knows this guy fucked up. All I can hope is that he gives him shit about it after I leave. Not that I believe it'll change this guy's attitude. I just want someone to give him shit.

I walk out the door figuring that I'm lucky to get away with just a fourteen-dollar fine for T-shirts I already owned.

UNIVERSITY POLITICS

"I've seen the Gus Van Sant films that you worked on and I'm not a fan. I hope that doesn't offend you," said a hip young film instructor who teaches at a prestigious east-coast college.

Why should that offend me? They aren't my films.

Moses and I are at a conference for film and video instructors in Texas and I'm not in a good mood.

I ask about his work. He's making a little experimental short that I "probably wouldn't understand." I didn't hit him but thinking back I probably should have. And it wasn't finished yet. Apparently none of his films are finished, except his student work, which got him his job.

Why the fuck is this guy teaching if he hasn't completed any films since his student work? And the worst part is, he's not the only one.

Over the years I've watched a lot of films by students and faculty, and as bad as some of the student films are, the faculty films are often worse.

Not always. I know some faculty who are great filmmakers but they're few and far between. Unfortunately the wrong people will read that last sentence and think I'm talking about them.

Many university film programs are grabbing unqualified teachers straight out of school (their schools) and putting them in classrooms to teach students something in which they have no real experience. But then the instructors are cheap and that's really all the schools care about.

Many schools open up film programs because, "It's what students want." Oh yeah and they can be cash cows for the university. They're selling a dream that all of these graduates can be filmmakers and have successful careers and make lots of money. And we all know that isn't going to happen.

There are too many places that teach film/communications/digital media or whatever you want to call it. And there aren't enough good teachers. And if a department is full of Ph.Ds, that usually means they don't know shit about making films, at least in my experience. There might be some Ph.Ds who are good filmmakers, I've just never met them.

There's a disturbing trend in higher education where a degree is worth more than actual work experience. Ph.Ds can be great at writing about films or critiquing films and telling you all sorts of wonderful things about film history, but teach production?

Like Woody Allen says, "Those who can't do, teach. And those who can't teach, teach gym." I've sat through a lot of lectures by people who shouldn't be allowed to teach gym either.

Students have told me about "professors" giving assignments and telling them to go on to YouTube to learn how to use the editing software. Really? I'm paying a lot of money to a school and the person teaching the course doesn't know how to use the software for the class? I want my money back!

I DON'T CARE ABOUT THE 'OLD DAYS'

I'm listening to a panel at a student-run film festival at Appalachian State University where Moses and I are appearing. I was on the panel before this one and have to do a workshop after.

This panel consists of three faculty members from the film department. These old dudes are not listening to the moderator, a student. Mostly they're telling stories about the "good old days" when they shot film. Right now, I envy Moses sleeping in the van while I'm listening to this crap.

One student asks about social media and developing fan bases for their work. The oldest professor who's been doing most of the story telling blows off the question. "Students don't have fan bases," he says chuckling.

Another student states that because of the Internet their films are being watched, liked, and commented on by people all over the world, so they are building fan bases. The professor scoffs again ignores the question and goes off on another of his stories from the "old days."

The students have to put up with this bullshit, but I don't. From the audience I jump into this debate and take the student's side. I make a point about how filmmakers have to develop fan bases to get their work seen. This old guy looks at me like, "Who the fuck are you?" He's about to find out.

I call out the faculty on what they're teaching and how technology and the marketplace have left them and their methods behind.

One professor states that he makes films for the local PBS affiliate so he understands the marketplace. I ask him what the affiliate pays for his work so the students will have an idea about what they can expect if they do something for PBS. He gives his films to the station for free!

I gracefully point out that he's *fucking* other independent filmmakers by giving his films away for free. He's also teaching the students a lie that they can make money. People who give their stuff away really piss me off.

I'm sure this PBS affiliate doesn't feel the need to pay local filmmakers for their work because of people like him who get regular paychecks and don't have to rely on making money from their work to live. I have dealt with these kinds of stations. It's bullshit. They have no problem paying for other shows that they air but they won't pay for work by independent filmmakers. And Ken Burns doesn't count. On any level!

The panel discussion suddenly becomes lively. The students are pelting the faculty with questions that they can't answer because they've never had to make films for a living, not in the last thirty years anyway. I should also point out that I've been to all of the screenings at this festival and haven't seen a single faculty member at any of them. My guess is they don't care. They get paid really well to show up to teach and that's all they're going to do.

This panel finally finishes and there's a twenty-minute break before my workshop on marketing and self-distribution. I leave to walk Moses and clear my head. When I return and start my workshop I see all three of these faculty members have stayed. During the workshop two of the faculty ask questions and actually take notes. They come up to me afterwards and talk.

The oldest member of the faculty does not. And even though the other two faculty members claim they want me to come back and speak to their classes next time I'm in the area, I never receive an invitation. I feel bad for these students.

Moses and I do a screening and a workshop at the University of Iowa organized by a group of film students. Since the school has a film department I send emails to some of the faculty saying I would love to meet them. I'm also happy to come and talk to any of their classes since I'll be there anyway.

No one replies.

I do the workshop and screening and it goes well. The students who attend are happy and take me out for dinner to continue asking questions. I ask about the faculty not returning any of my emails. They're not surprised. They told the faculty that I was coming and they were totally uninterested.

Apparently whenever they bring filmmakers to campus the faculty rarely attends. That tells me what kind of a film program they have, if the faculty isn't interested in meeting other working filmmakers.

Now here's the deal. Maybe as a lecturer I suck. Maybe the faculty is afraid that if they offer me an invitation and I turn out to be bad then they'll look bad. Or maybe they think I want to teach there and I'll be hitting them up for a position.

None of those things are true. And whenever I send out emails offering to teach I always include references so they can check me out and find out that I do know my stuff.

In my experience, real filmmakers are always eager to meet other filmmakers. You never know if someone can help you out on something you're working on or perhaps you can help them. Apparently that's not true with many academics who may or may not be tenured but obviously don't give a shit.

I found out about a professor at one university who had done his thesis on Gus Van Sant's remake of *Psycho*. I approached him but he wasn't interested in having me come and lecture. In fact he never even spoke to me about his thesis and I was the sound designer on that film. I would think he'd be interested in talking to me just for stories about what we did, never mind that I had worked on a film years ago with one of the sound editors who worked on Hitchcock's original film. And he told me all sorts of cool stories about the original.

I would think that if somebody sent me a note wanting to come speak to my class, I would take the time to check them out and see if they have something interesting to bring to the table. If not, I would at least contact them and say, "No, thank you."

Apparently, if you're an academic at some schools, you don't need to be courteous or professional.

I HAVE BILLS TOO

I get asked all the time to come and speak for free. When a university or college tells me they have no money, they can kiss my ass! I have a kid in college and I know how much I pay in tuition. They have the money. They choose not to spend it on guest lecturers.

These schools expect me to pay my own way to their campuses and to tell their students about my experiences working in the film industry. If you asked any of these faculty if they would teach for free they would look at you like you're crazy and yet they expect people like myself to come in and do it. If you asked anyone not in the arts to work for free they would also look at you like you're nuts.

"It's only a few hours," they tell me. It's not. It's twenty to thirty years because that's the time it has taken me to acquire the experience and the knowledge that you want me to give away to you and your students for free.

It bothers me that my time and the time of other artists is not considered important enough to be paid. And I see this over and over again. I have a family and bills to pay just like anyone else. I have worked hard to get to where I am in my career and I expect to be treated with respect.

There are other people or things they'd rather spend it on, and those things usually have more to do with what the faculty wants than with giving the students a well-rounded education.

One of my friends at a small religious school always has me come and talk to his students. He always gets me an honorarium. He went to USC after I did and since I've worked on some larger mainstream films he thinks it's important that students get a different perspective about the business.

He has some good students and once they get over the fact that I swear – a lot – we have some great discussions. And for the record I try really hard not to swear too much. Sometimes I'm successful. Sometimes I'm not.

At the end of every semester, he always asks his students what their favorite class was. They invariably tell him, "We love the guy who swears. We learned a lot from him."

More and more I see schools reflect the egos of their instructors. Some faculty are more interested in getting a steady paycheck and going to conferences than they are actually teaching students real filmmaking skills. And too many teachers want to be friends with their students. What the hell is up with that? When I was in school you always knew who was in charge and we never socialized with faculty. Ever!

I feel bad for students who are paying way too much money and not getting anything for it. In my opinion fewer than 10 percent of all of these students will still be working in film or in a media related field ten years after they graduate.

No scientific data, it's just my experience and what I've witnessed over the years. And Moses would probably agree.

ON-RAMPS, FUEL STOPS, and REST AREAS

On the road you're in your own world. I turn on music, drive in silence, contemplate the universe, and I talk to Moses. He's the best travel companion and I'm probably a better human being because of him.

Moses affects everything I do on the road. I'm always mindful of the temperature, and check to see if he gets too hot or too cold. I stop often to let him out and stretch his legs. There are times when he's not feeling well and I take care of him as much as he takes care of me.

Overall he's a low-maintenance dog but every now and then he gets sick. And he usually can't wait until it's convenient. There are times when I'm hurtling down the highway and he starts whining. Moses is not a whiner, and certainly not a complainer. Whining means, "Pull the damn van over because I need to relieve myself, one way or another."

Over the years I've stood on the side of more than a few busy highways as he gets ill. A couple times I've pulled over when it hasn't been the safest thing to do, but if I don't get him out of the van quickly it's going to get ugly and there will be a mess.

Because of this when I see other animals on the road I'm much more sensitive to their plight.

Outside of Ashland one morning we're filling up with gas when I notice a guy on the freeway ramp holding a sign asking for money. On the ground next to him is a big dog.

As a rule I don't give money to healthy looking people standing on the side of the road, especially if I see them smoking cigarettes. Dude, if you have enough money for smokes you can afford food.

While my van's being filled up (no self-service in Oregon) I open up one of the roof boxes and grab an extra bag of Moses' food. I walk over to the guy at the ramp and hand it to him.

"Take care of your dog and he'll take care of you."

I know if I give him dog food, the dog will eat. If I give him money, who knows? I'm a sucker for dogs, and kids.

As I walk away I hear, "No one's ever given me dog food before. Thank you."

FUEL STOPS

I'm filling up at a truck stop in Ohio when a thirty-something fat guy in shorts and flip-flops walks up.

"Hey man I'm stranded and trying to get home. Can you give me twenty dollars so I can put gas in my car?"

How many times have I heard this one? And the people who use that line are almost always full of shit! They say their car is blocks away or some such nonsense and basically they just want the cash.

"Not today."

The guy wonders off and I hear him ask a few other people. They all say the same thing.

I go inside to relieve myself. As I'm walking back out to the van, I see the guy leaning against an old beat up Chevy Suburban with a tired looking woman and three small kids. The kids look hot and dirty. I walk over.

"Is this your family?"

"Yeah."

"You out on the road with three small kids and you run out of money? What the fuck are you thinking?"

As a father I'm pissed. It's one thing when you're single and out on an adventure, but to be out on the road with small kids and begging for money? And from the looks of their car they aren't living in it, but close.

He looks at his feet.

I know some people have some bad luck from time to time. Hell, I've been there a lot. But somehow I don't see myself just asking for money. I always try and figure out something, some way to make it work.

Seeing the little kids gets to me.

"Pull your truck over to that pump next to my van."

I don't say anything I just put twenty-five dollars worth of gas in his tank. I'm not all, "Have a nice day" or "Good luck!" or anything. I'm pissed that he would put his kids in a position like this.

He mumbles a thank you as I get into my van and drive off.

To this day I don't know if it was a scam or not. If it was then I hope he rots in hell. And if it wasn't then I hope he made it home and some day down the road maybe he'll remember what I did, even if I was an asshole, and he'll help someone else.

REST AREAS

I'll admit it's weird to roll into a rest stop and experience *déjà vu*. After a while you start looking forward to certain rest stops.

The first rest area in most states is the "Welcome to Our State" rest area that has all sorts of information about the state and usually free coffee. These are the good ones, usually staffed by retired people, and they want to help.

Some of these places are huge. You step into the rest room and it's bigger and nicer than the ones at stadiums for big sporting events. They're always clean and since they're staffed you feel relatively safe.

The worst rest area is on Interstate 80 in Nevada. It's disgusting! There was shit and flies everywhere and yes it was hot, but it looked like it hadn't been cleaned in weeks. It was disease central. And it wasn't just one stall, it was every stall. The state of Nevada should be ashamed of itself.

Given the state of our economy these last few years, a lot of rest areas have people begging for money. Sometimes if it's a family, I'll drop a couple dollars. If it's a single person I'm less likely to help, unless they look like an old veteran. A lot of times I'll chat with some of the old guys. It's a good way to make them feel like humans and that they matter. On occasion you get to hear some interesting stories.

On a sunny day we pull into a rest area. There's only one other car there and it's parked far away from the restrooms. It's a late-model foreign car, maybe ten years old, and it looks in good shape with fancy tires and wheels.

Laying on a blanket outside the rest room is a young good looking guy, mid-to-late-twenties, sitting next to a sign asking for money. He's wearing shorts and a tank top and he's sunning himself. His tan seems to be coming along nicely.

He asks for money as I go in and out of the restroom. I say I can't help him today and he looks annoyed. I get Moses out of the van and we walk around for a while. For once we're not in a hurry.

More cars come and go and they ignore this guy. I see him say a few things but it doesn't seem to be helping his cause. The guy appears to be getting upset, so naturally I can't leave. I need to see what happens. It's lunchtime so I hook Moses' leash to a picnic table give him a biscuit and put his water bowl in front of him. I make myself a sandwich.

All the while I'm keeping an eye on this guy. He continues to ask people for money but they are just not buying what this guy's selling. He looks too good to be begging. He's in good shape physically and he doesn't appear to have a story about car trouble or anything.

Finally I see the guy get up, grab his sign and blanket and walk down to the late-model Acura with the expensive wheels that I saw earlier. He throws his stuff into the trunk and pulls out a cell phone.

I watch him animatedly talk to someone and he's pissed. I'm not close enough to hear the conversation, but as a public service I'd like to offer him some advice: If you're going to beg for money you should at least look like you need it. Multi-tasking, like working on a tan while you're asking for money, isn't a good idea. You should also have a few props like extra clothes and maybe some small dirty children. I can't guarantee success with this advice but it'll certainly work better than what you got going there.

SO WHERE IS *ORAGONE?*

It's funny, people always want to strike up a conversation with me at rest areas, gas stations and restaurants the farther I get from home. They love to comment when they see my license plates.

"Oragone. Boy you sure are a long way from home…"

"Yes I am."

Or…

"What's the weather like out there?"

"I'm not sure, I'm here." They looked disappointed so I add, "It's probably raining though." That seems to make them feel better.

"Oragone, is that near California?"

"Yep. Head straight west and hang a right at Bakersfield. You can't miss it."

"Did you really drive out here from Oragone?"

How do I respond to that last one without sounding like an asshole?

And yes, they rarely pronounce the name of the state right. I stopped correcting people years ago. After visiting Versailles (pronounced VER-Sales), Kentucky, I realized that it just didn't matter.

I MUST LOOK REALLY SCARY

There are few things worse than having car problems on the road. If my low-tire light comes on I get stressed and pull over as quickly as I can. I also carry a small compressor just in case. Yep, I'm that paranoid.

It's really hot as we're driving through Indiana. Moses and I roll into a rest area to take a break. I prefer parking far away from the rest rooms. It feels good to stretch my legs between the van and the restroom. Plus the dogs-only areas are usually on either end of the rest area.

I notice a late-model car with its hood up and a young woman sitting inside. Leaning against the car is another woman, I'd guess they're both college-age.

The women look at me as I walk by but say nothing.

Heading back out toward the van I hear the woman leaning against the car asking an older man passing by if he has a spare can of oil as their oil light has come on. The person avoids her stare and shakes his head as he walks past.

I let Moses out and we walk around. Yeah, we rarely stay in the dogs-only areas. If I don't see any employees that work at the rest area then I just go wherever Moses leads. On the way back to the van I see the women are still there, the hood is still up and people are walking past not making eye contact and shaking their heads.

How bad must I look if I'm the only person in the rest area they don't ask for help?

In the van I always keep tools, extra coolant and water. I used to carry motor oil but not anymore as the van never needs it. I do have an AAA card, just in case.

I open the tailgate and grab two bottles of water. Moses and I go over to their car and offer the women water. The one outside the car reaches down and pets Moses as they graciously thank me.

They're headed back to college and their father had checked over the car before they left. The oil light had come on and when they checked the oil it wasn't showing on the dipstick. They're about a hundred miles from school.

I've passed through this area before and I'm familiar with it. I volunteer to take one of them up to the next exit, which is about twenty miles away. There's a truck stop there and we can buy a couple of quarts of oil and bring it back. I figure one of them should stay with the car, just in case.

They look at me for a moment and then look at Moses. The one that was outside the car says she'll come with me and the other agrees to stay with the car. I think they both figured that any guy with a big old dog is probably okay.

When my daughter started driving I got her a AAA card and told her if anything ever happens, call me first. If I'm not around call AAA and stay in the car until someone arrives.

As a father myself, I would be nervous if I found out my daughter had accepted a ride from a stranger. Actually I'd be a lot more than just nervous.

I know they're taking a chance, one of them getting into a car with a stranger, so I tell them to feel free to take a photo or write down my license plate number.

Then off we go. We have a nice conversation about college, what she and her sister are studying and what I'm doing out on the road. After driving by myself for so long it's nice to have a conversation, even if it's only for a short time.

At the truck stop I tell her to buy at least two quarts of oil but three would be safe. She buys three.

Back at the rest stop I wait while they pour the oil into the car and start it up. There's oil showing on the dipstick, the oil light is off and so I wish them a safe journey and off they go.

I still want to believe that if someone breaks down it'll be good people who stop to help.

I still find it interesting that the one person they were avoiding making eye contact with is the one that helped them. Yeah, I know I look pretty scraggly sometimes.

A PERFECT NIGHT for DRINKING with HANK WILLIAMS

It's a beautiful warm spring night in Montgomery, Alabama. We're up on a hill far enough from the city that the sky is loaded with stars. Moses and I are hanging out with new friends. We're drinking beer, eating food, and listening to some great live music. The singers and musicians include an author, a journalist, a Ph.D candidate, some attorneys from the Southern Poverty Law Center, a graphic designer, and a woman who's introduced to me simply as "an heiress." She's looking quite relaxed on xylophone.

They're playing Hank Williams tunes and most everyone in our group is singing along. It's one of those joyous, relaxing nights after a great screening. When the music pauses, the night is still. It's quiet up here. Like a cemetery.

Which makes sense because we're in a cemetery. In fact I'm sitting right in between Hank Williams and his wife Audrey.

And they're not saying much.

I just finished playing a small art house theater in Montgomery. The theater owner found a local couple that is letting me stay at their home while I'm in town.

Jim and Trish have become life-long friends. Moses and their dogs, Amos Moses and Bear, become their own little pack. Okay, maybe "little" is the wrong word as they're all big dogs. Jim and Trish contact friends and arrange a meet up after my screening of *The Gas Café*. And when you're in Montgomery, where's the best place to meet up for beers and music? The cemetery.

Apparently this is a tradition. Have a beer with Hank Williams around midnight, since Hank died around midnight on New Years Eve in 1953. No one cares that New Years Eve is supposed to be the night that you do this, any night will do.

Now there is a huge celebration every New Years Eve. It's a giant party up at the gravesite with Hank Williams impersonators and fans. People come from hundreds and thousands of miles away to celebrate. But that's another story that Jim will be telling at some point.

Trish has made up a nice light supper and brought a blanket to lay it out on. Other friends arrive with beer, wine, a bottle of rum (not a good idea) and musical instruments.

We talk, we eat, and we drink.

The conversation starts with film and music but soon turns to race and politics. These are fascinating conversations and no one is shouting or interrupting. If people disagree they wait until the other person has finished. Wow, civilized discourse on these subjects. I can't believe it.

I ask questions about the type of work every one does, (except the Heiress, as that seems rather obvious).

I learn a lot about the Southern Poverty Law Center and their mission. I hear about death threats and moving forward with cases whether you're afraid or not. I learn about the history of Montgomery and things about the civil rights movement that weren't taught in my school. I learn more about Hank Williams than I ever thought I needed to know. And the great part is that these people I'm with are storytellers. They bring this stuff to life.

I'm sure the rum and the Heiress' musical accompaniment help.

There is a great tradition of Southern storytelling that I love. Some of my favorite writers are from the South. They have a way of telling a story that puts you right there in the middle of it. Their stories are rich with details, and the details are what make it a story. I could go on for pages about Southern story telling but please find books by Rick Bragg, Pat Conroy, Fannie Flagg, Carson McCullers, Flannery O'Connor, and of course Mark Twain. There are so many more, but I'm going to stop here and get back to our story.

I look up at the clear night sky and realize how lucky I am. Moses and I are a couple thousand miles from home and we're welcomed and accepted by this group of strangers who have all led pretty interesting lives. Some of these people have stood up for injustice and have fought for the rights of people who can't always afford to fight for themselves. It was a phenomenal evening. One of those nights when being on the road is a great experience.

We're there for a couple hours, maybe longer. Don't worry, we finished up all of the alcohol, even the rum.

SEEING SOME OF THE CIVIL RIGHTS SITES

Jim arranges a tour the following day of the Southern Poverty Law Center.

To me, the civil rights movement in the U.S. was something that occurred far away in time and place. I was born in 1956 so while people were marching for their rights in places like Alabama and Mississippi, I was still figuring out how to tie my shoes.

I was also in Oregon, and by design we had very few African-Americans in the entire state. But that's a different story, a different history.

I had no firsthand knowledge and it's only through extensive reading that I found out about the civil rights movement in Oregon. And it wasn't until much later that I learned that Portland had "sundowner" laws through the 1950s. You see, in Oregon we pretend things like this never existed out here.

In the morning Jim takes me to the Dexter Avenue Baptist Church and explains its history to me. This is the church that Dr. Martin Luther King, Jr., led from 1954 to 1960. I saw him on TV and in film clips leading big marches. I never thought that he also lead a congregation. I also didn't realize that he was in Montgomery, I'm not sure where I thought he was. I probably never thought about it.

From there we go to the bus stop where Rosa Parks boarded the infamous bus and we walk the short distance to where the police pulled her off the bus. It's a humbling experience to be where history happened. The spot looks nothing like I imagined, especially on a beautiful spring day.

The first thing that catches my attention at The Southern Poverty Law Center is that the building sits off the street and the landscaping is done in such a way that no vehicle can get close to it. Jim explains that there have been so many threats against the attorneys here, that the building has been designed so that no car bombs or other types of incendiary devices can get close.

I'm lucky enough to get a sneak preview of their new exhibit hall that's going to be opening the following week.

Learning about the people who fought and died in the civil rights movement is important. There is no way, especially for a white kid in Portland, Oregon, to relate to these struggles. I've seen news footage and documentaries about the marches and the fire hoses and the dogs being turned lose on the marchers, but to me and I'm sure to many others it's just history. It took place a long time ago and in some other place. I've always looked at it with a certain historical detachment.

I can't do that here.

This exhibit puts a human face on the struggles, especially the faces of the children. These images are burned into my brain. Reading the stories, seeing the photos and being in a place where you can focus on this is life changing. You can't look at the civil rights struggles the same as before you walked in. At least I can't. I'm moved. History has come to life and it has come to life through the faces of children.

Coming here was the most moving experience I've ever had on the road. And it took quite a bit of time after I left Montgomery to truly process what I saw and what I learned. I have the utmost respect for those who fought and died in the Civil Rights Movement.

ON A LIGHTER NOTE

One evening Jim and I and the dog pack are sitting in the backyard. We're enjoying cold beers and leftover pizza. Moses appears at my side and in one fluid move pulls a slice of pizza right off my plate and disappears. By the time I catch up to him it's totally gone.

I've always been very strict with Mo as far as his diet. I don't allow him to beg or eat human food, especially when we're at the table. There is nothing worse in my mind than a hundred-and-twenty-pound dog that begs. Or steals food off the table.

But Moses is older now. He doesn't move as fast as he once did and he sleeps a lot more. I'm older too and I think about all of the adventures we've shared. He isn't going to be around forever. Once I would have disciplined him and let him know how unhappy I am with his behavior.

Now I look at this old guy and he knows what he just did was wrong, but he enjoyed that slice. I reach down and pat him on the head. I tell him not to do that again in a very soft voice. I go back to my beer and the rest of my pizza. Moses comes over and lies down at my feet.

Yeah, he's a good one.

IT'S NOT ALL GLORY... HOLES

I'm doing a screening in Tulsa at the Nightingale Theater. This place is best known for live (experimental) theater but every now and then they book films. Amber, Jeff, John and Sara have put their heart and soul into this place and have always taken chances when it comes to live theater. It's great to hang out with people who are so dedicated to their art and craft that they figure out a way to make it work. Plus we always have a good time when I come by.

I've been there numerous times and on this trip I'm doing two nights.

Before the first screening, I'm booked on a local television show to promote the event. I show up and the place is in a frenzy. It's tornado season. Tornadoes are expected all around the area over the next few hours. One lands about fifteen minutes away from where we're standing.

My interview is canceled. Apparently they feel public safety and reporting on disasters is much more important than me doing shameless promotion for my show. So we go to the theater and wait. No one shows up. This is not good for my fragile psyche. Oh, fuck it! It's just the weather.

Taking this news in stride, we walk around the corner to a local bar. This place is a last stop on a descent into severe alcoholism. Or it's a way station. I'm not sure which. Locals will tell you it's a gay bar, and not one of those fancy decorated places. This bar is a dump with glory holes in the men's room. The patrons all seem to be drunk, dirty and will never be on the cover of *GQ*. But alcohol is cheap and since it's walking distance from the theater...

My friends know the bartender well, but that doesn't stop a lot of the toothless, drunk-ass patrons from coming over and trying to start conversations with all the guys. I know, these guys are just looking for a little love, or fresh meat. I'm not sure which. But we're all straight and I'm just trying to drown my sorrows over my canceled show and the fact that I'm not making any money tonight.

The females in our group have a conversation with the bartender and she makes it quite clear to her regulars to "Leave those folks the fuck alone! They're friends of mine." Which is appreciated but really only serves to slow them down a bit.

We proceed to get pretty drunk ourselves and after one of the guys in our group reports to us about getting aggressively hit on in the men's room, the women take it upon themselves to escort us to the women's bathroom and wait outside the door whenever nature calls our names. It's an interesting night but without incident.

The next morning we hear that there was quite a bit of tornado activity in the area but the danger seems to have passed so I am hopeful for tonight's screening.

THERE'S ALWAYS ONE GUY...

Tonight I show my film *Kicking Bird* and quite a few people show up. It's not going to make up financially for last night but I'm always grateful that anyone shows up. Now if they'll only buy some merchandise afterwards that'll be great.

While the film is playing Moses and I wander around the neighborhood because, well, I've seen it. Plus Moses always likes to check for his scent at places we've visited before.

It's always weird when you're doing a Q&A afterwards and someone asks you something that just stops you cold.

"So how would you like to be remembered?"

Where the fuck did that come from? After a while you figure out comebacks for just about anything and I don't skip a beat on this night.

"Do you know something I don't?"

The audience laughs. But he keeps asking questions.

Most of the people leave after the Q&A, except for one couple. Yep, the guy who asked the bizarre questions. After so many tours you can tell pretty quickly who the "interesting" ones are. They have the crazy eyes.

He continues to pepper me with "questions" and then tells me about his brother, a big Hollywood actor. He thinks the two of us should work on something together and his brother can get it made. I can direct and he and his brother can star. As usual I point out that I don't live in town and besides I'm pretty busy right now. This doesn't deter this guy at all. He is already making plans for our success.

I take all of this in stride until I find out who his brother is. *Gary Busey!* The guy who was in the motorcycle accident and plays all of the crazy guys in the movies. He later had his own reality series, *I'm With Busey*. And who could forget when he did *Celebrity Rehab with Dr. Drew*. Yeah, *that* Gary Busey!

If this guy is half as crazy as his brother, I'd be afraid to even go on the set. I politely tell him it sounds good and I'll think about it, but I need to take my dog for a walk right now, and I excuse myself.

He stays and talks to the theater owners for a while. He's a regular who tries to engage any visiting artist the same way he did with me. My friends tell me later that he's pretty harmless. Right.

THE KINDLY GRANDPA KICKS MY ASS

Whenever friends would have screenings and Q & As back home, we'd always show up at the screenings with a couple questions ready to ask even though we knew the answers.

There's something about getting that first question that feels like it takes forever. You're waiting, as seconds feel like minutes, and you just want someone to ask something! Once that first question gets asked then the rest come faster. I don't know why, but that's the way screenings always go. So we were always prepared with questions to help our friends out. When you're on the road you usually don't have friends in the audience with that ready first question. And trust me, the first question always dictates how the entire Q & A is going to go. If it's a good, friendly question you're going to have a good night. If hostile, not so good. And I've been there.

There must be three hundred people in this theater in Chicago. The place is almost packed. I've never done a screening here and I'm amazed.

This whole screening has been put together by a fan. I met a wonderful fellow via the Internet who had seen some of my work and decided if I wanted to come to Chicago he would host a screening at a local theater. And he'd give me all the proceeds. Wow!

He and his wife were wonderful. I stayed at their house, they had two small children, and had dinner with the rest of his family. It was great. One of the nicest couples I have ever had the pleasure to meet.

And the screening he put together was amazing. He did all the publicity and organizing and even paid the rent on the theater for this screening. I still can't believe how many people showed up.

The audience went crazy at the end of *Kicking Bird* as I walked up to do the Q & A. I thanked my hosts profusely and thanked the audience for showing up. Now it was time to take some questions. I see half a dozen hands go up right away. This is going to be good.

I spot a gray-haired distinguished gentleman just a few rows back. He's well dressed and has that whole nice-grandfather-full-of-sensible-advice thing going for him. Why not start here?

The dude ripped me a new asshole!

Overall he liked the film but there was one shot toward the end that reveals what I think was an important character flaw. He hated that shot! He felt it was totally unnecessary and, man, he really went off. In a nice grandfatherly way, but he went off.

The entire theater was quiet. Now what?

I addressed his question head on. I told him I disagreed and that we had even done a couple rough-cut screenings of the film without that shot and the audiences didn't understand it. They didn't think that character was such a bad guy. But when we added that shot in he was definitely a bad guy and the audience turned on that character. I made the decision that we had to keep the shot in.

I was calm, respectful, and I gave him the real answer as to why I put the shot in. I thanked him for coming to the screening and for his question.

I turned to the rest of the audience and said, "Okay, next question?" And not a single hand went up. This guy's question took all the energy out of the room. I'm not sure how long I waited until I finally got that next question but it felt like a lifetime.

It took three or four questions before the energy level in the room finally returned and I was working hard to get that energy back. A few people commented afterward about Grandpa ripping me a new asshole. I told them straight up that I appreciated his honesty and actually was looking for him afterward to talk to him more and to thank him again for coming but I couldn't find him.

When you do things like this you have to be ready to deal with whatever comes your way and you have to do it respectfully, and hopefully with humor. Whether someone likes your film or not, you can't come off like an asshole.

But I will admit that now when I see a grandfatherly type at one of my screenings I don't necessarily call on them for the first question.

WHEN YOU LEAST EXPECT IT

"I'm sorry sir. Your credit card didn't go through."

"Excuse me?"

"I tried it twice. It was rejected both times."

Everyone at the table is looking at me. I offer to buy dinner and this happens.

"That can't be right, I used it for lunch today and there's at least $500 on that card."

"I'm sorry sir. Do you have another card?"

I pull out cash. I always have travel money on me so it's not a big deal. I have enough to cover the check. Barely.

I've been on the road for a month and still have another month to go. I go back to where I'm staying, get on-line and check my bank account.

Shit! It's been wiped out.

I call the 800 number for my bank. I tell them I'm in Texas and I have no idea why there are two charges from Delaware on my account. Did I mention this is my business account? The one I use to track all of travel expenses?

"Wow, you're really quick. These charges haven't even gone through yet."

"I checked my account earlier today. I check it at least once a day when I'm on the road."

Lucky for me those two charges haven't gone through yet. The woman on the phone is able to reverse them. I get my money back. Then she cancels my card.

I'm really fortunate. I was in Houston the day before finishing up a large job for Michelle, a friend of mine. She was going to make a deposit directly to my account that day but I tell her to do it when I come back on Friday because I'm in a hurry to get to Austin. If she'd made that deposit I would have lost a lot more than $500 and I'm not sure how nice the bank would have been to me.

The woman tells me that they'll send out a new card with a new account number in seven-to-ten days.

Wait a minute? Seven-to-ten days without my debit card? I'm on the road. What the hell am I supposed to do?

I have very little cash and no access to my business account for seven-to-ten days? And they'll only mail my new card to my home address. They can't forward it to me on the road. She's sorry but those are the rules. If they send the new card anywhere but my home address then it could possibly be a scam. How do they know that it's really me they're talking to? I get it but what a fucking hassle.

I have a feeling I'm going to be sharing Moses' food with him for the next week.

I'm also convinced because of the timing of this that someone at the restaurant I was at earlier in the day ripped off my number. I'm ready to head over there and raise hell!

A fellow from the bank's fraud division says it could have happened anywhere. One of the most likely places was probably a gas station. Since most gas stations around the country are self-service (except in Oregon and New Jersey) it's easy for someone to slip a reader into the card slot at the gas pump and make off with lots of credit card numbers and no one is the wiser.

I head back to Houston and explain what happened to Michelle. She's amazing. She gives me part of my money in cash. I send the rest back to Portland to be transferred into my business account (which is now secure) and then have a friend make a transfer of some of the funds to my personal account so I have enough money to pay bills and continue the tour.

CHRIST, UFOS, AND ALIEN ABDUCTION

Have you ever seen Christ of the Ozarks? I hadn't even heard of it until I was booked to do a screening and a workshop in Eureka Springs, Arkansas. One of the residents took me out on to the balcony of my hotel and showed me where to look among the trees and sure enough, way off in the distance was a giant statue of Jesus. And when I say giant, I mean seven stories tall. Is it a good statue? I'm no art critic but I did read one who said it was similar to "a milk carton with a tennis ball stuffed on its top".

Which I tend to disagree with. The head is really square. I'm not sure what the hell it looks like but I wouldn't have thought "tennis ball." Plus, the arms are extended out straight so instead of feeling like they're welcoming you it's like they're nailed to the cross but there is no cross? It's pretty strange.

They do a big performance of the *Passion Play* there in the summer. It's located in a religious theme park.

Eureka Springs is a beautiful town and in the summer it's quite the tourist destination. I met some wonderful people. But this town also attracts some interesting people.

After my screening and Q & A, this fairly normal looking woman comes up. She reminds me of an old hippie, only clean. She has some interesting insights about my work and wonders if I might look at a script she's written? I tell her I can't. Since I write and make my own films I can't really look at other people's scripts on the off chance that I'm working on something similar. And if I am she can come back and sue me, blah, blah, blah.

She understands and is happy to sign a release as she really thinks her script would be of interest to me. I have no releases on me. She gives me her business card. I glance at it, can't believe my eyes, I shove it in my pocket to look at later.

After a few more exchanges, she leaves.

The last guy there is someone I'd met earlier. We have mutual friends. He offers to help me break my stuff down and maybe we could grab a beer. I'm all in.

As we're drinking, he asks if I had taken a good look at that woman's card yet? I pull it out of my pocket.

"You've seen this?"

"Oh yeah. She gave me one when I first moved up here and did a screenwriting workshop."

I look at the card again. It has the usual name and phone number and then a list of her services. Her skill set includes,

Hypnosis, Past Life Recall, Spells Broken, Light Binding, Curse Removal, and my personal favorite, Soul Retrieval.

"Is this some sort of joke?" I ask.

"Did you agree to read her script?"

I shake my head.

"I did."

He was smiling.

"It was the weirdest damn thing I've ever read. UFOs, alien abduction, body probing, all sorts of really strange stuff. It didn't make a lot of sense and it was a mess. So I made all of these notes and had written up some things about structure and put together what I thought was some good feedback. I was new to the area and I really wanted to help her with this."

"And…"

"We meet for coffee and before I can say anything she moves in close and says quietly so no one else can hear, "I just want you to know that everything in that script is true. It all happened to me just like I wrote it down."

"What'd you do?"

"I slipped the screenplay and all my notes under my leg and told her that I really liked the story and I didn't have a lot of comments about it. We talked a bit about alien abduction, I finished my coffee and I got outta there."

Wow! I've dealt with some crazies, but that's major league.

NOT a FIT NIGHT OUT
for MAN nor BEAST

My hands are tight on the steering wheel and I'm concentrating. Moses is snoring and I'm praying I don't hit something or someone. I'm praying that I'll hurry up and get through this zero-visibility fog. I know it'll be this way until I drop down below the summit and I'm sweating bullets.

I got a late start. I shouldn't have met my friend Bruce for lunch in San Francisco but I haven't seen him in years and it was good to catch up. It's six-thirty now and I'm starting that long climb through the Siskiyous. It must've rained recently. The road is wet, a little slippery, and very dark.

It's the end of another fall tour and the last hurdle I have to face is the Siskiyous, a small mountain range in northern California. In mid-November I'm never sure what the weather is going to be like here, which is why I always get an early start out of the Bay

Area. I hate driving through these mountains at night. Unless I want to sleep in another motel I have no choice.

I hate fog, especially at night when I'm tired. There isn't much traffic, which isn't a good thing. I'm about an hour from Siskiyou Summit and then the drop down into Oregon. An hour of thick fog and tired eyes.

On a flat stretch of highway I come up on a semi doing fifty-five. I decide to stay behind him for as long as I can. Which will probably be until the next long grade up hill where he'll slow down to twenty-five.

Passing in fog on a winding highway is the worst. You go from the safety of following a set of taillights to the unknown. In a few minutes we hit the next long grade and he starts slowing down quickly. He's probably got a full load.

I check my mirrors, see no one behind me, so I make my move. I veer to the left and am immediately blanketed. I can see the semi to my right and I try using his headlights to see beyond my own. Nothing but white. I accelerate around him and pull back into the right lane as soon as I can. I turn on my high beams. They illuminate the fog. I can see less. I turn my headlights back to normal.

I'm trying to remember exactly where I am as I climb. Is there a drop off on the left side of the road? I have no way of knowing. I keep one eye glued to the hazy white sheet in front of me hoping to spot something out beyond my headlights. The other eye is on the white stripe on the right side of the van. I don't want to miss a turn in the road and find myself plunging off into who knows what.

Why is it that when I'm driving in weather like this I turn off the music? Am I afraid listening to music might impede my sight? Or do I feel I have to concentrate on the road one hundred percent and any distraction will send me to my doom? But shouldn't music calm me, make it easier to concentrate? Fuck if I know, but I keep the music off anyway.

Moses is oblivious to my stress. I hear him licking his paws.

I'm straining to see road signs, how many miles until Hilt, or to Ashland? Hilt is just below the summit, Ashland is at the bottom and that should mean visibility. Unless the whole valley is fogged in too.

I'm the only person on this planet and this planet is fucking scary. I want to be among other cars, trucks, and people. I want to feel less isolated, less alone. Even if we're heading straight toward a cliff there's safety and a feeling of security in numbers.

I'm passing the exits for Weed now. The fog is thicker.

I'm six hours from home and after two months on the road my bed is calling.

Why is *Radar Love* stuck in my head?

I'm not sure how good of an idea it is, but I pass the last Weed exit.

If I can make it to Yreka and the fog is still this thick I'll pull off. Yreka's in a flat area just south of the last long hill up to the pass. It might be clear there for a few miles. I think there's a Motel 6 there.

Suddenly the thick white veil is broken by light. Headlights. A Chevy pick-up screams past me. My speedometer says I'm doing fifty. The Chevy is going at least seventy-five.

Drivers like this amaze me. Do they know something I don't? Can they somehow see better than I can? Or are they just in a hurry and don't care?

The fog encloses me again as the tail lights disappear quickly into the milky white mist. I don't like this.

I think of Ken Kesey's book, *One Flew Over The Cuckoo's Nest*. Chief Bromden, the narrator of the story is crazy, and whenever things get stressful he talks about the fog settling in around him so he can't see anymore. I'm starting to feel like the Chief and I'm worrying about my sanity.

After what seems like hours, I come up on a set of taillights. Another semi. I glance at my speedometer. He's doing thirty. I brace myself and go around. I'm hoping that another lunatic like the one in the Chevy doesn't come flying up my ass.

There's another semi. Fuck, I have to pass two of them! I'm gripping the wheel tighter, like this is supposed to help?

As I pass the second semi I see the last exit for Yreka go by. Shit, how did I miss Yreka?

Not that it matters. I've passed it now so I have no choice but to keep moving forward. Soon I feel the road dropping down, descending? We haven't reached the summit yet have we? Did I miss it? What the hell?

Oh yeah, the highway drops hundreds of feet before it starts to climb again toward the summit. Even during the descent the fog doesn't let up.

During the day I've marveled at the amazing engineering feat that is Interstate 5 through the Siskiyous. Tonight I just want to get through it. I just want to be home.

I feel the road start to climb again. I'm heading for the summit. It's a long stretch and I remember there are steep drop offs on my left. Now it widens to three lanes. I can make out a group of semi trucks with their flashers on to my right, slowly climbing the hill. They're maybe doing twenty-five miles an hour. I see trucks on the shoulder going even slower.

I remember moving back to Portland from LA years ago pulling a packed trailer with my old Toyota Land Cruiser. It was June and the sun was beating down. It was well over a hundred degrees. That old Land Cruiser was barely doing twenty miles an hour struggling up this final hill. Semi-trucks were passing me. I wish I was back in the Land Cruiser right now. It doesn't go fast, but it always felt safe and sure.

Up ahead a semi has merged into my lane to pass another semi. He might be doing thirty-five. I have to decide whether to jump into the far left lane to go around. This is the area with the big drop off. I'm pretty sure there's a guardrail. I still can't see shit. Where's the summit? I've gotta be close.

I take a deep breath, check my mirrors one more time and go

for it. I glance at my speedometer, forty-five, fifty, fifty-five, sixty, sixty five...

I race past the semi and slide back into the center lane. I'm breathing hard like I'm pushing the damn van. There, off to my right I barely make out the "Welcome to Oregon" sign. I'm almost to the summit.

Moses gets up, moves around, and lies back down in a different position. He scares the hell out of me! I forgot he's back there.

There are two more semis but they're in the far right lane. My heart is racing, all I can think about is the summit. I just want to get over it. All will be okay when I start heading down the other side. Please let me get over this...

I feel the road flatten out and know off to my right is the truck pull-out where trucks can check their brakes before the six-mile descent. The fog is thicker but it doesn't matter – I'm almost on the down hill side. I feel the cold sweat on the back of my neck. It's dark and cold and foggy and I'm sweating.

Three lanes become two and I see a truck slowly merging into my lane with its flashers on. I can't see a fucking thing behind me, but one more time I slide into the left lane. I know I'm close to where the highway starts descending and now the drop-offs are on my right. The road is wet and I realize it might be slick. I can't tell if it's icy or not. We're up over four thousand feet. Please don't be icy.

When will this nightmare be over? I'm so fucking tired. My neck is tight and my head is pounding.

I pass the semi and start the six-mile descent. Is the fog getting any lighter? I can't tell. Shit, what if the whole valley is fogged in?

I'll stop in Ashland if it's still foggy. I don't care anymore. I just want to get out of the fog, get outta the van.

I move in and out of the left lane, as the semis are all going down the hill slowly with their flashers on. Most are doing thirty miles an hour, or less. I don't want to stay in the left lane because you never know what's going to come up behind you. I remember the runaway truck exits are down here somewhere. The pavement is dry now but it still feels treacherous.

Two more cars go screaming past me. My eyes are dry from staring straight ahead. The muscles in my neck are bulging.

Suddenly the fog is gone! It doesn't thin out. It's just gone. I see the valley stretched out in front of me. The lights of Ashland are beautiful, and it's clear.

My body starts to relax. Just five more hours behind the wheel and I'll be home.

I accelerate to seventy. Another fall tour is in the books.

SPRING WEATHER IS ALWAYS UNPREDICTABLE

Moses and I are cruising along Interstate 40 through Arizona. It's cold but sunny. I'm not sure what the elevation is as I'm heading toward Flagstaff but I can feel the cold through the windows. It's a busy stretch of highway. I'm trying to remember the last time I saw so many trucks. They feel like they stretch for miles in the right-hand lane. I've been following a black BMW for a couple of miles doing a very comfortable seventy-five. There's an Acura right behind me.

As I'm passing another semi, all of a sudden clouds are overhead and it literally starts snowing! The snow is dumping down on us fast and it's thick. Where the hell did this come from? Everyone starts to slow down but no one slams on their brakes, thank God. No one I can see anyway.

I want to change lanes and get over into the right lane and slow down but a double trailer semi is there. I'm right at the mid-point of the two trailers. Either I have to slow down and let him get past or I have to speed up and get around him. There are trucks in the right lane as far as I can see, there's no way I'm getting over.

The snow comes down harder, it's building on the road quickly. I can't see the pavement at all. Suddenly the BMW starts to lose control. It starts fish-tailing in front of me and it's also right next to a semi. Visions of him hitting the semi and taking me and a lot of other vehicles out with him flash through my mind.

Oh my God! This BMW does a one-hundred-and-eighty-degree spin and his front end is staring at me. My foot is coming off the accelerator but I'm not hitting the brakes. I know it's slick as hell and if I lose control I'm fucked.

Suddenly the BMW spins again and he is able to turn his car so he shoots off on to the shoulder as I go zipping past him. I'm not sure how much room there is between us, but it isn't much.

My hands are gripping the steering wheel with everything I've got and my eyes are riveted to the road in front of me. I check my speedometer – I'm doing fifty. That truck is still right next to me, a quick glance in the rearview mirror tells me the Acura is still right behind me. The snow is coming down so thick I've already lost sight of the BMW.

How the fuck do I get out of this? I don't. I can't. I have to hang on and drive to the best of my ability. I'm suddenly very happy the van has front-wheel drive. I can't see the pavement, I have no idea how deep the snow is but the van is tracking straight and true. I just hope the back end doesn't lose its grip.

And suddenly I'm out of it! It's sunny, the pavement is bone dry, and it's like none of this ever happened. I've heard of flash floods but a flash blizzard? WTF? But that's what it was.

I pull off at the next rest area, which is only a few miles down the road. I need to catch my breath. Moses and I get out and he heads straight for a large bush and pees. We walk around for a few minutes as I attempt to relax. Like I said, it's sunny but it's cold. We jump back in the van and as I am pulling out of the parking lot I see the black BMW pulling in.

This little episode gives me a real appreciation for long-haul truck drivers.

I grew up around rain. Rain doesn't bother me. I spent my youth walking to school in it. We'd go camping in the rain. Rain happens year-round in the Pacific Northwest and you grow up learning to deal with it. I can remember it raining on my birthday some years and that's in the middle of July.

In Oregon it can rain for days. It doesn't usually rain with any force, it just keeps coming down until it soaks everything. That's not what happens in the South. When it rains there, it comes down in buckets. It pours to where your visibility is zero, or less.

I spent four hours one day behind a semi driving through Tennessee and all I could see was the back of the truck. That's not totally true. At times I could see cars and trucks in the ditch to my right, sometimes upside down. It's a nerve-racking experience driving in storms like that. But if you have bookings you have to get there.

The only time I ever didn't make it to a gig was one spring in Grand Rapids, Michigan. Because of the snow. The streets were so slick I wasn't sure I could get to the venue. Since I was going to be there for three straight nights we decided to cancel the first night and hope for better weather.

The next afternoon we went to the venue and there was a note on the door from three guys who had driven forty miles from another town to see me. It was probably pretty treacherous for them to get there, but they did. And they were greeted with an empty building. No one had put any signs up as far as canceling the gig because of weather, nothing. I felt like shit letting them down.

I've never canceled another gig because of the weather.

THE ONLY GOOD WIND IS A TAIL WIND

Driving through Colorado and Wyoming I hit a huge head wind. I don't know how strong it was but I was literally wrestling the steering wheel.

The van averages twenty miles a gallon on the road. Today I'm getting twelve. I can feel the wind grabbing the roof boxes trying to shove me backward. My foot is literally pushing the accelerator to the floor.

I pull into a truck stop to refuel and give my body a rest. My shoulders ache, my hands are sore, and my neck is a giant knot. I need chocolate.

Getting out of the van I fight to stand up. The wind is whipping around and large objects are zooming past me. I look to the sky to see if a house or a spinster on a bicycle is flying by just so I can say, "Moses, I've a feeling we're not in Kansas anymore."

This wind goes on for eight hours and two tanks of gas. By the time night falls I'm four hours behind schedule and physically exhausted. I find a motel and Moses and I sleep soundly. Although I should point out that Moses has been sleeping pretty soundly the entire day.

The next morning my shoulders are killing me, but two Advil later and we're back on the road trying to make up time.

The 2005 Ford Freestar is not the most aerodynamic vehicle ever built, especially from the side. Where did they even get that name, Freestar? The van is shaped like a brick. Add a roof rack and two roof boxes and you have a recipe for instant and unexpected lane changes at a moment's notice.

Once again, there's not much you can do about it as you're always expected somewhere and there's no time to sit back and wait for the wind to stop.

WYOMING? NOT A FAN

One spring driving through Wyoming I experience all weather. The eastern side of Wyoming starts off with thick fog, the almost zero visibility stuff. After what feels like hours I get out of that and it starts snowing. Hard. I get through the snow and it clears up and is sunny for about a hundred miles. Then it gets icy. I slowly work my way through the ice and into a huge thunder and lightning storm with heavy rain. Did I mention that now it's dark?

By the time Moses and I roll into Salt Lake City I'm a basket case. I'm stressed out and just want to be home. I've been on the road for seven weeks and I can't take it anymore.

After three years the spring tours come to an end. I can't do them anymore. All because of the weather.

I BLAME YOUR PARENTS

On the road I meet a lot of students who want to be writers and directors. Their parents have told them they can do anything they want.

YOUR PARENTS ARE WRONG! You can't do anything you want because most of you have no work ethic! (I won't even talk about talent at this point.) And would it be politically incorrect to mention that some parents procreate stupid offspring?

You think what we do is easy? And cool? Well, it may be cool but it's certainly not easy. I've taught classes and workshops in high schools, colleges, universities, film festivals, media art centers, you name it.

Here are a few things I've observed;

Most students don't read. I'm not saying they can't read, although judging by what they write, my guess is they don't read well. I can't tell you how many times I've been confronted with, "I didn't do the reading for today, why don't you just tell us what was in the book so we don't have to read it?"

How stupid do you have to be to take a class and ignore the reading assignment that is from the book that the instructor wrote?

And, no! I won't tell you what was in the reading. You need to do the work yourself.

So many students want to be writers and they don't read books or even screenplays. And some of them are proud of the fact that they don't read. What's up with that? All great writers have been readers. You can't learn how to write without reading – a lot. For whatever reason, these young people think writing is easy and that a first or second draft is good enough to shoot. I won't show draft five or six to my family and they love me. Once again I'm going to blame your parents for telling you that you're a good writer. They have to tell you that, they're your parents. And they're wrong.

Writing takes time and discipline. You have to work at it every day if you want to be any good. Every day! There are no shortcuts.

By the way, you don't have a photographic memory. Take notes! If you don't take notes and you screw up, that's on you. (I also see this with interns.)

SIZING UP THE STUDENTS

When you're waiting for a class or workshop to begin, you learn a lot about the students as they file in. Who sits in the back? Who's talking? Who's with friends? And who sits front and center?

By and large those who sit in the front row think the workshop is all about them. They'll talk while I'm talking, make comments, and ask questions that aren't really questions but comments intended to show everybody how smart they are. They aren't.

When I was in school, if we found out there was a guest coming to speak, we went to the library and did our homework. There was no way we were going to be embarrassed by not knowing who they were and what they'd done. Before I go to film screenings, if the filmmaker's going to be present, I look up their work so if I have the opportunity to meet them I wouldn't embarrass myself by my ignorance.

Even with smartphones, most students are so self-involved that they don't take the time to look up anyone else.

At one school I called out a kid who was interrupting me while I was talking. I use the term "kid" loosely. He was probably in his mid-twenties and at that age he should know better. He thought that being funny and the center of attention was more important than the rest of the class hearing what I had to say.

After being interrupted for the third time I told him to either shut up or get the fuck out! The instructor got really uncomfortable when I said this. The kid didn't say another word until after class when he came up and apologized. I accepted his apology and he asked me a couple of very good questions. Then he thanked me for coming.

Obviously I've never been asked back to that film program.

WHAT AM I, THE ANSWER MAN?

Some students not only don't listen, they don't participate except to tell me that they know more than I do. I ask questions and they expect me to give them the answers. That's bullshit.

I start calling on people. I point to them and say, "What do you think?" One kid said, "I'll pass on that question."

That's never an option. If you think you can get out of my question with a funny comment, you're wrong. Give me your best guess or I'll keep coming back to you until you at least try to answer the question.

And for those people who are shy, and I can usually spot them, I will compliment and be as supportive as possible if they're trying. *My goal* is to get students to think, not embarrass them.

Here's another exchange I've had many times in the classroom:

"John, you got your assignment?"

"No. But it's not my fault."

"It's not your fault?"

"I had to help the seniors with their project."

"Are you in their class?"

"No but they needed help and I stayed up all night to help them finish so I didn't get my assignment done for this class. So it's not my fault that my homework isn't finished."

"So you made a choice? Do the assignment for my class or help other students on an assignment for a class you're not in?"

"Yeah."

"Then it is your fault for not getting the assignment for this class done."

"No, it's not my fault. I had to help to them."

"Were they holding a gun to your head?"

The class laughs and he shakes his head.

"You had a choice. You chose not to do the assignment for this class even though you knew it was due. It is your fault for not getting it done."

"I just said it's not my fault."

"But it is. You need to take responsibility for not doing the assignment and the grade that will come from your decision. And that will be an F."

"That's not fair. It's not my fault."

"You keep saying that, but it is your fault. You need to own your decision. Let's move on."

These students don't get it and many of them never will.

I have students complain that they hate using a particular piece of software for an assignment. I tell them that this software is the standard in the industry and if they want to work in the industry (which is why they're in this program, I'm guessing) they need to learn how to use it. Then I hear how it's hard to use and they already know another program and why can't they use it instead. They will spend a lot of time fighting me on this.

"Frankly, Scarlett, I don't give a damn!"

If you wish to be a professional in this business you need to learn this program now or you can do it later after you've been rejected for jobs because you don't know it. Do the homework as assigned. I don't give a shit if you thank me or hate me later.

And what the fuck is up with parents contacting the schools and complaining on behalf of their kids? I've heard of parents complaining about teachers, curriculum and grades. In sixth grade my daughter wanted me to go talk to her teacher because she didn't agree with a grade she got on a paper. I told her that if she wanted to get the grade changed then she needed to write down all the reasons why and give them to her teacher and ask for a meeting to discuss the grade change. Why should I do it? It wasn't my paper. We worked on her reasons together and then she gave it to her teacher and asked for a meeting. Her grade was changed for the better. She did it herself and continued doing it her entire academic career.

If a parent ever calls me to ask for a grade change on behalf of their kid, I'll ask them why they're calling. It's not their grade and if their kid doesn't have the guts or care enough to come see me themselves, then there is no way in hell I'm changing their grade. Get out of your kid's life!

My favorite students are the older ones, the mature ones. Many of them are going to school part-time because they have jobs and families and realize this is what they really want to do. Some are ex-military.

What the older students have in common is they want to learn. They pay attention, take notes, and ask really good questions. I like these folks.

The ex-military students are interesting because they want you to be specific with the assignments. They want to do it right the first time and they don't want to disappoint you. In the beginning when I give them general assignments where they have to be creative, they struggle. They've been in a system that has told them to follow orders, don't question and don't fail.

I tell students they'll learn a lot more by taking chances and failing than by doing what is safe and expected. I hate safe and expected. It's okay to fail. In fact, I love it when they fail especially if they took chances. We go over why they failed and how they can improve. When I see the lights come on, that's the best feeling.

Many students think their work has to be perfect. If that comes from your parents then *your parents are wrong* again. Everything you do in life will not be perfect. Not even close.

Why am I the one who has to tell students they're not geniuses?

As students, you need to fail. You need to experience difficulties and setbacks. I know I've failed. More than once.

I've said this before and I'll say it again: I lost my home of twenty years because I failed. I listened to the wrong people, got bad advice, and it cost me. I screwed up my life big time. And I learned from that.

I've had to start over and rebuild my business and my life. I had to admit my mistakes and accept full responsibility for my actions. I believed other people and they didn't have my best interests in mind. They had their own interests. I worked my ass off to help others hoping they would do the same for me. They didn't. And my parents didn't bail me out. I suffered the consequences. And it made me a better person and a better filmmaker.

It is because of my failures that I started touring in the first place. You need to embrace your failures. Learn from them and move on.

IF YOU CAN'T TAKE THE HEAT

You have to have your work thoroughly critiqued. I know, your work is perfect. It's interesting, a lot of people think their work doesn't need to be critiqued, but they're more than happy to critique everyone else's?

If someone critiques your work they're critiquing something you created, not you personally. Leave your ego outside and listen. You might learn something and you might become a better artist.

You have to develop a thick skin if you want to be in a creative field. Your parents are doing you no favors by telling you everything you do is great. It's not!

Over the years Moses and I have spent too much time in classrooms where students aren't learning for a variety of reasons.

I blame parents who don't get involved with their kids and the schools. I blame parents who don't read because children learn by example. And I really blame parents who raise their kids to play games where they don't keep score and everyone gets a ribbon because there are no losers.

There are losers! And losing is important. How else are you going to know if you're any good or not? You learn from losing and you improve from losing or you find something else to do.

Fuck you, parents! Let your kids fail. Don't always make everything easier for them. Let them see what the real world is all about. You're not doing them any favors by being overprotective. Why should I be the first one to tell them their work and their attitude sucks?

Kids, stop listening to your parents when they tell you how good you are. They're lying. You need to have a good work ethic and practice your craft over and over. No matter what it is. And maybe after a few years, you might become decent. To become great requires a lot more effort.

HELLO BOSTON!
(Or is it CLEVELAND?)

Moses and I have been on the road for well over a month. In the past sixteen days we've done a workshop or screening every day. Throw in a daily two-to-three hundred mile drive to get to those gigs and yeah, I'm feeling pretty ragged.

I'm not a big rock star but I do get confused. And no, it's not drugs, alcohol or all the groupies. It's the relentless pace of being on the road and making a living. And since I'm not a big star with my own tour bus and driver, it makes everything harder.

Moses and I are doing a workshop at the Mindframe Theaters in Dubuque, Iowa. It's our first trip here. We pull into town, meet the people who're sponsoring the workshop, and after a pleasant dinner head to the theater.

There are forty people tonight, a good crowd. I allow the organizers to film portions of the workshop but they're not allowed to show or post any more than five minutes of it. I've got to protect myself.

Although I'm tired, I've always prided myself on doing the best job I can do, whether it's for two people or two hundred. Tonight's no exception. I find a second wind, or a third wind or whatever, and I'm on fire doing my *Extreme No-Budget Filmmaking Workshop*. The audience is into it and the questions are good. I'm informative, funny, and feeling great.

I get through all of the information and there's still time left. I ask if they want to talk about other things like self-distribution or film festivals? They eagerly say yes so I talk for another twenty minutes.

The main organizer has to leave early so he's not around when I finish up. The audience crowds around the merch table and continues to ask more questions as they buy stuff.

Finally it's time to start loading out. I'm looking forward to heading to my hotel and sleeping because I have another three hundred miles to drive tomorrow. Moses and I will be up early and on the road. A couple volunteers come up to me with copies of the posters that were made for this event.

Volunteer: "We saved a couple of these to give you for your poster collection."

"How sweet! Thank you so much. I've seen them around but haven't had a chance to look at them."

I look now.

Oh my God! I have just spent three-plus hours doing the

wrong workshop.

It's right there in front of me. I was supposed to do my workshop on *Self-Distribution and Film Festivals*. I did the *Extreme No-Budget Filmmaking Workshop*.

And no one said a single thing to me. I'm so fucking embarrassed.

The next morning I call Joe, the organizer, with the revelation that I had done the wrong workshop and he burst into laughter.

"You knew?"

"I figured it out about twenty minutes in, but you were on such a roll and the audience was right with you that I didn't want to interrupt. I figured I'd just invite you back next year and you could do the right one."

Joe made good on his word and he and others in Dubuque have invited me back multiple times. And I've never made that mistake again.

In fact, I have five more days of workshops and lectures and lots of driving in between so I start my lectures off telling the Dubuque story as a reminder to myself to confirm with the audience that I'm doing the right workshop.

TAKING A DAY OFF CAN PAY

It's freezing and raining and I'm not feeling well so I stay an extra day in Iowa. I just want to be warm and stop moving for a day. I'm also not feeling very sociable. I'm sure Moses wants a break from riding in the van.

I nap or spend time on my laptop getting some writing done. The heat's cranked up. The TV's on in the background, which is odd because I rarely watch it. As I work familiar music comes on. I know that tune. What the hell is it?

That's my fucking commercial!

I turn and watch. It's a commercial I directed for a bank in Oregon. A humorous spot featuring a woman and a dog at a lake. The dog gets so excited that he knocks the woman into the lake. The spot did really well and I think it might have even won an award or two. So what the hell is it doing on TV in Iowa with a different bank's logo on it?

I write down the name of the bank and shoot off an email to the creative director at the agency who had written and produced the spot.

He reminds me that we were approached by a syndication company that sells pre-shot commercials to clients who can't afford to make their own. We agreed to syndicate a couple of our spots in return for a percentage of whatever they sold the spot for later.

This was done a few years earlier and we both forgot about it.

This company told us how excited they were about our spots and were sure we'd make some decent money on them. And we never heard from them again.

They were contacted the following day and back-pedaled like crazy. They assured us that they had tried contacting us but hadn't been able to find us. We both still had the same phone numbers and email addresses. Liars!

They eventually paid us a decent sum, which we split. Imagine the odds. I'm on tour in Iowa, take a day off, and just happen to have the TV on a channel that's showing this spot. Wow!

I've often wondered how many times they'd sold this commercial or the other one and kept all the money?

What a great fucking business.

FUN FACTS TO KNOW

The downside of driving so much and going to so many places is that you become dependent on your GPS. There are some places it doesn't help you and the faster you figure it out the better.

In some cities my GPS is always about ten feet behind me. I don't know why but it is. As I'm navigating the friendly voice will tell me to make a turn on the street that I've just passed. Her timing couldn't be worse because I'm usually in traffic. Then I'm berated and told to "Make a U-turn, make a U-turn," until I can finally find a less risky alternate route.

Apparently GPS units are not always familiar with the local laws.

SOMETIMES THE GPS DOES LOOK AFTER ME

I just finished a show at Pittsburgh Filmmakers and I'm driving back to my motel when we get hit with a snowstorm. In late April! Like I need this.

There is absolutely no traffic on the freeway and I can't see anything, especially the white lines. This will teach me to stay for one more beer when I'm told that a storm is coming in.

I need the GPS to get us off the freeway at the correct exit and back to our motel. I can't see the exit. I can't see much of anything. I'm relying on that suddenly reassuring voice to make sure I don't end up in a ditch.

I'm not a snow expert and I am certainly not going to take the time to get out and measure, but it feels like there's already six inches on the ground and it's still pounding down.

I can't even see the exit when I'm told to get off. I move slowly and am using the small posts that are sticking through the snow as my guide. I crawl up the exit and I still can't see anything until I see the stop sign at the top.

Once again thank God for front-wheel drive! The van has yet to slip, but then again I'm not going very fast and I'm running this damn stop sign. I don't see any other fool driving so I slowly push through it and make a left.

We make it back to our motel and Moses and I fight the snow and wind to get into our room and hunker down for the night. Moses takes the fastest pee I've ever seen him take so he can get out of the snow and into the motel room. He's not happy. It's not that he doesn't like snow, he does. He doesn't like the high winds blowing it in to his face. I'm wondering how the hell I'm going to get to our next gig tomorrow.

We wake up in the morning and almost all of the snow is gone. It's like the storm never happened.

THE AMERICAN DREAM

When I interviewed the writer Studs Terkel in 1986 he talked about a coarsening of society. We're no longer civil to one another. Well, Studs, if you thought it was bad in the eighties, just look around and see where we are now. It saddens me that we can't have calm and intelligent discourse in this country.

One night in Texas some friends I'm staying with invite a few of their friends over for dinner. We sit outside enjoying a warm evening and cold beers. The talk turns to politics and I'm blown away how quickly the conversation gets heated. Some people are vehement in their beliefs. There's no room for discussion. I'm right and you're wrong. And just like on TV they have no problem interrupting and shouting others (mostly me) down.

We can't have a discussion. It's their way only. Worse yet, they attempt to brow beat me and another person into submission. It was important that we agree with them (like that was going to happen...). They wouldn't listen to our points and cut us off in mid-sentence. I wasn't able to finish a thought.

It disturbs me that an actual political discussion couldn't take place. I've always politely listened to others and then politely disagreed with them. I've found over the years that the more you shout and cut people off, the more holes your argument usually has.

In *Travels With Charley*, Steinbeck writes about the ugliness of segregation in Louisiana on his cross-country trip and the things that people were screaming at the child attempting to enter school. He talked of being sickened at this display. With all due respect to Steinbeck, it may not be as blatant but I think it's worse.

Politicians and the media are instilling fear in us and are actively working to divide us. There is an attitude of, "if you're not for everything we're for then you're against us and have no right to be Americans! Get the hell out of here!"

I still remember the whole "My country right or wrong!" and "America: Love it or Leave it!" from the Vietnam era. Many years later we're not any smarter and we're still going down that same road. There is a divide in this country that has been getting wider since the 1980s and it shows no sign of lessening. People have no interest in other people's points of view and compromise is looked on as a weakness. The Internet has given us people who can say what they want under an assumed identity and I've read some incredibly harsh things.

I used to think we were better than that. Now I'm not so sure.

I've seen what's considered news sources and it's anyone with a serious sounding name, a blog and an axe to grind. There's no fact checking, only misleading headlines. People only read what they already believe in, they look for views that confirm their own. Often times they repost articles that they haven't taken the time to read but they agree with the misleading headline. And then, by God, look out! They spew this stuff as if it's fact.

Real journalism is a thing of the past. With media companies owned by huge corporations, the major concern is bottom-line profit. Once television news became subject to ratings just like the entertainment divisions, any objectivity went out the window. It's all about packaging stories to sell to us. Twenty-four-hour news channels have given us nothing but pundits, pretty faces, and people trying to cash in on book deals for books people buy but don't read. Newspapers are scaling back or shutting down all together and they're hiring fewer and fewer people with any kind of journalism background. And all of this media is everywhere we turn.

I'm so fucking tired of other people telling me what to think.

Over the years I've met thousands of people on the road. They come from all types of backgrounds and have many different experiences. I love listening to their stories. I felt the need to start talking to people and since I'm traveling around the country anyway, I might be able to get a better idea of what's going on than all of those assholes on TV, radio and the Internet.

So for a couple years I took a camera with me and talked to people.

I focused on the phrase the "American Dream" because it's become a catch phrase used to sell everything from houses to lifestyle. "These people are living the American Dream. This is the American Dream. The American Dream is what we all strive for."

But what is it really? I asked four simple questions:
- What does the American Dream mean to you?
- What do you think your parents thought the American Dream was?
- Is it still possible to achieve the American Dream?
- Do you have any other thoughts on the American Dream?

Simple and straightforward.

On the road I started off by talking to people I already knew. Then I talked to people I met at workshops, schools, coffee shops and motels. I didn't just stick a camera in people's faces like all these news shows do. I'd strike up a conversation, get a little of their story, and then ask if I could film them.

Some people were reluctant to answer my questions thinking they might give me a wrong answer. I assured them there are no right or wrong answers I just want their thoughts. My goal was to get as many people from different walks of life as possible. I did this on a couple different tours.

WHAT DID I FIND?

Many people told me The American Dream is freedom. When I'd ask them to elaborate, I heard things like freedom to pursue your dreams. Freedom to travel, to live the way you want, to be yourself. We can do anything because we're free.

I often heard that we were the only country on earth that was free. (My apologies to my friends in Canada, Europe, and many other countries – apparently you're not free.)

Freedom is an ambiguous word. What does it really mean? Well according to the dictionary:

Freedom – *noun* –

1. the state of being free or at liberty rather than in confinement or under physical restraint;
2. exemption from external control, interference, regulation, etc.;
3. the power to determine action without restraint;
4. political or national independence;
5. personal liberty, as opposed to bondage or slavery;
6. exemption from the presence of anything specified (usually followed by from): freedom from fear;
7. the absence of or release from ties, obligations, etc.

When you look at these definitions, I wonder if any of us are truly free. Certainly many of us are not in confinement or under physical restraint but are we really free from all external control? We have limited power to determine our own course of action because we have laws in place to protect ourselves and others. We're not slaves in one sense, but if we have mortgages, credit cards, and debt, aren't we slaves to the banks and other corporations? We all have some sort of obligations and ties to those around us.

All of our decisions are made factoring in all of the above. So are we really free? I think there are degrees of freedom but for so many people to use that word as a blanket statement says to me that they don't truly understand the concept. They aren't free! There are always things that restrict what you can and can't do. That's the way any society has to be set up.

There were quite a few people that stated that the American Dream was to have a family and to have them close to you. Oh yeah, and to have a really nice house.

People in the twenty-to-thirty-five-year-old range talked about the American Dream as a materialistic thing. It was about owning things, having a large house, a new car and the latest stuff. These young people, whose families had been here for generations, were all about owning as much as possible

There were some who were against accumulating things and having this false sense of ownership. They weren't buying in to that. They talked about travel, having experiences, and pursuing their individual goals. They talked about personal growth and helping others.

One of the common threads as far as their parents were concerned, they believed that home ownership and comfort was what their parents wanted. They wanted to be wealthy.

It was the first and second-generation citizens that thought the American Dream was about education and opportunity, to build a better life not for just themselves but for their families as well. They talked about knowledge and how education can make a difference in your own life and you could also make a difference in other's lives.

They talked about hard work and sticking together as a family so that they could send their children to school. They were making sacrifices for their children so their children could have a better life.

The most interesting thing for me was that the non-white people I spoke with all had hope. They were upbeat and were actively putting in the work that would help them achieve their dreams.

A lot of the white people I spoke with were not nearly so upbeat. They tended to be much more negative about everything. Many of them spoke about not doing better than their parents.

So what did I learn from all of this?

I realized that the people who traveled, who had other experiences, and had seen other places, had open minds. It was those who were born and raised in the same area and didn't travel, even across the state let alone the country, were the ones that believed things were awful. They were the ones that were suspicious and close-minded.

I am reminded of Mark Twain's quote, "Travel is fatal to

prejudice, bigotry, and narrow-mindedness, and many of our people need it sorely on these accounts. Broad, wholesome, charitable views of men and things cannot be acquired by vegetating in one little corner of the earth all one's lifetime."

As a country we're still very much a melting pot and the people with good attitudes and hope are the ones that I believe will benefit from their own hard work. A lot of other people are going to get left behind and those that will get left behind will blame someone else for their misfortune, rightly or wrongly. And when we get a lot of people that blame others for their misfortunes we will see Americans turn on each other. And it's already happening. Look around.

I believe that education is the key to a better life and a better country, and if you stop learning then you stop growing. There are an awful lot of people I have come across in my travels who have stopped growing. And it's no one's fault but their own.

If you don't have dreams, or you don't actively work toward your goals on a daily basis then you won't achieve anything. And if you sit back and blame others for your own predicament then you'll never get anywhere.

So many people I meet on the road are hard working, decent people who want to make a better life for themselves and those around them, but the media and politicians are working just as hard to divide us and to create suspicion among us. We can't afford that.

Get out and see the world. Travel – and you'll do us all a favor.

THE FIONA TOUR

**WARNING!
THE CURRENT EXHIBITION IS OF A MATURE SEXUAL NATURE.
CHILDREN WILL NOT BE PERMITTED WITHOUT AN ADULT**

"How bad could this be?" I thought.

Fiona and I arrive at the gallery that's hosting my first event. There's brown butcher paper on all the windows.

The gallery is full of sex toys mounted on various objects. There were some things that I'd never even heard of, but seeing them in the displays gave me an incredibly graphic idea of what they were used for.

Oh man!

I look at my fifteen-year-old daughter. She's looking at the floor. Obviously embarrassed. Great! I can imagine her next phone call with her mother.

Fiona had been bothering me about a road trip so one summer we plan a three-week tour. Before we leave my ex-wife tells me she doesn't think the trip is a good idea.

"You know Fiona doesn't like change. She likes to be in her own bed every night. She's not going to like this."

Actually my ex is the one who doesn't like change.

All I say is that Fiona will be fine. Fiona tells me later that her mother and her mother's boyfriend have made a bet on how long Fiona will last on the road before she calls up in tears and asks them to fly her home. Needless to say, that doesn't happen.

Our first stop is a small contemporary art center on the northern California coast. I'm showing *Kicking Bird* and doing a Q & A. We're going to spend the night with a friend of the people that run the gallery. I'm supposed to call to set things up before we get to town and she'll come to the show. She's not answering.

Back at the gallery we're shown where to set up. Fiona sets up the merchandise table. We're surrounded by strange sex toys. She's very quiet. So am I.

We have time to kill so we take Moses for a walk around town. Fiona always refers to him as her little brother. She's very protective of him. It goes both ways. He doesn't like to let her out of his sight when they're together.

Down by the water we come across a bunch of drunk and drugged out street people who're yelling, fighting and making their presence known to everyone.

One big fucked-up ugly guy yells something at us. I really

don't want to be messed with and I'm hoping the sight of the big dog keeps them away. I can see Fiona's nervous. We keep walking.

Finally I say to her, "If you want to talk about any of the stuff that was..."

"No! I don't wanna talk about it. Let's not say anything about it to anyone."

"Including your Mother?"

"Especially Mom!"

"Okay. But if you ever..."

"Dad. Let's never talk about it!"

I'm fine with that.

All during the screening I'm trying to get hold of the woman we're supposed to be staying with. Still no answer.

After the screening and Q&A I finally get a call back. She's not feeling well and has been sleeping. She gives us directions to her house. It's after ten p.m. by the time we find it. Fiona gets the spare bedroom and Moses faithfully follows her in. I get the couch in the living room.

The next morning we head south. The goal is San Jose and the Winchester Mystery House. After waiting in line for an hour we go on the tour. Mrs. Winchester's husband invented the Winchester repeating rifle. She was nuts and was convinced that she heard the voices of all of the people who were killed by the rifle. The only way she could escape from the voices was to keep building on to the house. So she did. Twenty-four hours a day, seven days a week for twenty years. There are stairs that go nowhere and every night she slept in a different room so the spirits couldn't find her.

You can get the complete story online and, if you're anywhere near San Jose, it's worth your time to take the tour.

What also struck me about the tour is the wholesomeness of the tour guides. They look like extras from a Donny and Marie Osmond show. These people make the Disneyland workers look like derelicts.

Our perky guide tells us that most of the seasonal help are college students. In a quiet moment while others are looking at a bizarre staircase, I ask our guide what college she goes to.

"It's a school in Utah."

"Which school in Utah?"

She immediately changes the subject, which makes me think one of two things. She isn't really a college student (doubtful). Or my first hunch is right.

"Dad, they're Mormons."

"How do you know?"

"Look at 'em."

Fiona's probably right. I'm sure there are security cameras everywhere making sure that Fiona and I don't try to steal anything as we're easily the scruffiest looking people there.

We spend a couple days with friends in Santa Barbara and then down to LA. One of the reasons we're on this trip is to check out a few colleges for Fiona. Even though she's just a sophomore.

Fiona loves UC Santa Barbara. Who wouldn't? It's practically on the beach. In LA we go to USC where her mother and I met. Her mother is really pushing USC as Fiona's grandfather went there as well.

USC is located in a shitty part of Los Angeles and this fact is not lost on Fiona as we drive down Hoover Street. We take a side trip to see where I used to live off of Adams Boulevard, in an $85-a-month basement apartment. Fiona doesn't even want to get out of the car in my old neighborhood. I can't blame her.

We walk around USC and Moses pees on everything. There are times when the sheer size of his bladder amazes me. Long after he should be empty he finds a spot and dutifully marks it.

Now it's not that I don't like my alma mater, I do. I got a fantastic education there even if the physical environment was less than ideal.

Things have certainly changed over the last thirty years when the film school was located in a former stable. I think they're on their second set of new buildings since I graduated. It's amazing what *Star Wars* paid for. The buildings are amazing, as is the campus. It's unfortunate the rest of the neighborhood isn't. I've been told that the university is buying up land all around campus to make it safer and more appealing.

Fiona doesn't like the campus at all and who can blame her. It's in the middle of a noisy city and, although there are some trees and grass, it just doesn't feel like a traditional college campus. No matter how much lipstick they put on it, it's still a pig. And there aren't any departments that are of interest to her. She's happy to look around, but it only convinces her that she really doesn't want to go here.

A couple years later her mother fills out the paper work and submits it on Fiona's behalf. All Fiona has to do is write an essay for the application. It doesn't matter that Fiona has said over and over she doesn't want to go there.

She confesses to me later that she intentionally torpedoed the essay. One of the questions was something like, "What is the greatest invention of the twentieth century?" Fiona proceeds to use her entire word allotment on the amazing uses of soap. She tells me later, "Who ever reads this essay is going to think I'm crazy, there's no way I'm getting in."

When the letter arrives from USC, they do not accept her for the fall. They put her on a "waiting list." We never hear from them again. I love my kid.

In LA we stay with my old film school friends Tim and Leilani and their son TJ. We've always been close, but they've never met Fiona. Tim owns Area 51, a visual effects company and has worked on many great films.

Glenn Campbell, (no, not the singer) has worked with Tim for a long time. I've known him for a good twenty years but I haven't seen him in at least two years. Fiona and I walk into the office and Glenn, all six-foot-four of him is standing there. He doesn't say hello, he just looks right at me as if I had just been in yesterday.

"Is Superman a real superhero? The only thing that gives him super powers is the fact that on earth we have a yellow sun, on his own planet there's a red sun, and he's just an ordinary guy. So is he a superhero or not?"

Without missing a beat Fiona replies, "Well, Batman doesn't have any super powers, he's just a rich dude with a belt. Does that mean he's not a superhero?"

Glenn studies Fiona for a moment. Then looks at me.

"Your kid?"

I nod.

"She's cool. I like her."

Instead of being a typical bored, standoffish teenager, Fiona takes all this in stride. I have to leave her there for a couple hours to go to a meeting. While I'm gone Glenn shows her how to blow up a planet in After Effects.

We're driving through New Mexico and talking about school and some of her teachers. Fiona's reclining in the passenger seat. Suddenly she pops up and looks out the windshield.

In front of us is a wall of black clouds.

"Dad. What's that?"

"A storm."

"Are we gonna drive into it?"

I nod. "I usually hit something like this once a year."

"Are we gonna be okay?"

"I hope so. It looks pretty bad but we'll find out when we get into it."

"Can't we pull off somewhere?"

"We're in the middle of the desert. There's no place to go."

We pass the only overpass for miles and there are a bunch of cars packed underneath it.

"What about there?"

"There's no room and we don't know how big the storm is. We need to get to El Paso tonight. See that semi up there?"

I point down the road about half a mile.

"We're going to get up behind it and just follow it through this thing. It'll be okay."

I get in behind the semi just as we hit the wall of water. It goes dark, like it's night. The rain is dumping down in buckets and the visibility is lousy. All I can see is the rear lights of the semi. I hope he can see better than I can.

Fiona's pretty quiet as we drive through the storm. Within twenty minutes we're on the other side where it's warm and sunny.

The next night we stay with friends outside San Antonio. Fiona immediately feels comfortable with my friend Arati, who is a huge animal lover. Arati has two old horses, five or six rescue dogs, plus various cats she takes care of. Fiona helps Arati feed the horses. She's always been comfortable around animals.

Early the next morning Fiona gets her stuff together. She grabs Moses to take him outside to pee and put her stuff in the van. It's really foggy as she heads out the door. She's back quickly.

"Dad can you come with me?"

"Why?"

"It's really creepy out there."

"How can it be creepy, it's daylight?"

Then I remembered.

I go outside with Fiona and Moses. It's very early in the morning. The leafless trees are barely visible as the sun tries to break through the thick fog giving the area a ghostly feel. Slowly about fifty deer emerge from the fog. They're silent and staring at us as we walk. Some move closer, their large brown eyes fixed on us.

"See."

"Yeah, I forgot about this. If they get too close just let Moses off the leash, he's too slow to get any of 'em but he can spook 'em."

Fiona is hesitant.

"Don't worry, they're not going to hurt you."

"I know, it's just creepy. They're so quiet."

The deer follow us as we walk the twenty feet to where the van is parked.

Once on the road, I drive slowly through the fog. The visibility is lousy and I certainly didn't want to accidentally hit one. We finally get out of the fog and it's off to Houston.

Fiona witnesses first hand what a grind it is on the road, and she never complains. At one point she makes the comment that she couldn't figure out why I bought a minivan as we always made fun of them. Now that she's been on the road for a week she gets it. It's roomy inside and she can drop the passenger seat down so she can sleep, which makes early mornings on the road much easier for her.

We do two workshops in Houston and then on to Austin for two gigs over two nights. Fiona falls in love with Austin. And who wouldn't – it's a great town with lots going on.

After the second workshop we go to one of Austin's late-night diners for pancakes and beer. The beer is for me. It's way after eleven and Fiona's eating pancakes and looking around at all of the piercings and tattoos.

"Dad, this is so cool."

"Just remember, Kid, it's not all late-night diners and pancakes."

She knows exactly what I mean. She's already tired of people asking her the same questions at every stop. "How old are you? So are you going to be a filmmaker too? What's your favorite movie?"

She also tries to lecture me one night.

"You know, Dad, you tell the same jokes every night."

"I do. And I tell them in the same place, too."

"Well I'm getting tired of 'em."

"Are people still laughing?"

Fiona nods her head. "But I'm not."

"Sure, because you're with me every night, but the people who come see us aren't. These are all new jokes to them. I've worked on these jokes and their timing in the workshops for months and even years. That's why I know they work."

She thinks about this for a while.

"If you want I'll try to use some different ones tonight."

"No, if they work you'd better not mess with it."

Our last stop is the annual University Film and Video Association (UVFA) Conference in Denton, Texas. It's incredibly hot and I swear there isn't a single tree within a hundred miles. How do people live like this?

During the day while I'm at the conference, Fiona stays in the air-conditioned dorm room with Moses. She works on her computer and reads. In the evenings we go to the scheduled functions. It cools down enough so that Moses stays in the van while we're gone. I know it's boring and probably the last thing she wants to be doing, but she understands why I need to be here. I'm networking to line up more speaking opportunities for future tours.

I soon realize that most of the members have no interest in talking to me, and certainly no interest in inviting me to talk to their students. The professors I do know are great and keep introducing me around but there's a good-old-boy network here and I'm not going to break into it.

I'm pissed and frustrated, although I'm not going to let these fuckers see that. I make a phone call to my friend and marketing guru Margie back home.

"Why the fuck am I even here? These people are assholes! It's a fucking good-old- boys network. I hate this shit!"

"You intimidate them."

"Say what?"

"They're afraid of you because you really make films."

"So why are they intimidated?"

"Because they're afraid if you come to talk to their students the students will see that they don't know shit. They just talk about films. You make them, and you make good ones."

"I don't want to be here. I'd rather be hanging with Fiona."

"So tell yourself you're going to make five new contacts today and once you do that you can go hang with your kid."

"Five?"

"Five. And remember, you're the Angry Filmmaker. Fuck 'em! Be who you are and if you intimidate them then good for you!"

So I make five new contacts that night.

I skip out of the last day of the conference and Fiona and I explore Denton, which takes about ten minutes. We find a wonderful homemade ice cream shop and sit under an awning. Somebody needs to plant some trees around here.

It's an extremely long three-day drive back to Portland. Fiona and I are together in the van for three solid weeks and we get on famously. No arguments, or even disagreements. She's in charge of the music, and we talk about all sorts of things – except those weird sex toys at that museum.

Spending so much time with my daughter was a gift and I hope it went both ways. Seeing the world through her eyes and watching how she and Moses were joined at the hip was amazing. She was always concerned about how he was doing when the weather got hot and he was looking out for her whenever we went somewhere. He never let her out of his sight unless he got left behind in the van.

As my friends know, Fiona is very much her father's daughter. It's on this trip that I learn something else. She's just like me, but she's not me, and that's something that I always have to remember. She is her own person and I couldn't be prouder.

NIGHT MOVES

Ever feel like you're driving head long into a horror movie?

I'm winding through Ohio late one night (God, I drive through Ohio a lot), on my way to West Virginia. My GPS tells me to get off the interstate and take a small two-lane highway that will drop me down to another interstate that'll take me straight into Charleston.

I take the turn off and head south. The lights of the interstate dim in my rearview mirror and before I know it I'm on this dark, hilly, windy road. I'm listening to a compilation CD. Actually I'm not really listening to it, it's merely background.

As I get farther away from the interstate the road gets windier and windier. I slow down to forty-five, then forty, then thirty-five. There are no towns, no lights, and no traffic. The cheerful British voice on my GPS has said nothing for quite a while.

According to the screen I have thirty more miles before my next turn.

I pass multiple forks in the road while the GPS directs me to darker and darker territory. I check my cell phone. No reception. Not much of a surprise – I have AT&T.

I'm beat, but I push on. My eyes strain against the darkness. I'm scared to death that an animal or Sasquatch is going to jump out in front of me.

It's not raining but the clouds are eliminating any atmospheric light. I hit the high beams. The road is so twisty that even with my bright lights I can't see very far.

My mind races through the plots of every bad horror movie I've ever seen or read that involves a dark road in the middle of nowhere. The van has been running perfectly so why am I suddenly paranoid that it's going to break down?

Then I hear it – the voice, the scratchy sound. But it's the voice that's spooking me. It's Robert Johnson's *Me and the Devil Blues*.

I've heard this song a million times. I like this song. I even know the lyrics. So why is it that this song that I've heard over and over is now scaring the shit out of me? Probably because Robert Johnson sold his soul to the devil. I know it's not true but you listen to any of his songs by yourself late at night on a dark highway and then tell me you don't believe that story even for a minute.

I turn off the CD.

Never underestimate the power of music.

These are my five top songs that scare the shit out of me while driving late at night.
1. *Me and the Devil Blues* – Robert Johnson
2. *Brain Damage* – Pink Floyd
3. *I Put A Spell On You* – Screamin' Jay Hawkins
4. *Fire* – The Crazy World of Arthur Brown
5. *Radar Love* – Golden Earring (I don't need to hear that the driver dies in the end.)

And for the record I might as well give you a list of my favorite touring songs.
1. *An Old Greyhound* – Hoyt Axton
2. *Idol of the Band* – Hoyt Axton
3. *Shelter From the Storm* – Bob Dylan
4. *Thunder Road* – Bruce Springsteen
5. *Rudy Wants to Buy Yez a Drink* – Frank Zappa

What's on your list?

You would think that interstates would be okay driving late at night but it all depends on what part of the country you're in. When you're driving through Wyoming or climbing the Rockies, it's amazing how dark it gets out there. Interstate 80 through Nebraska goes on forever day or night.

There's always a time at night when it seems like even the trucks are off the road. All you can see is nothing but darkness for miles and miles. A moon is nice and what's even nicer are the lights of a town.

The thoughts that go through your mind late at night on the

road are the worst. I'm always afraid that suddenly someone is going to appear in front of me and I won't be able to stop. When the weird thoughts come flying through my brain or I'm stressed the first thing I do is turn off the music. Why? Does it help me concentrate when it's off?

I don't know, but I do it. I even do it when I'm trying to find an address.

Driving through Florida and the Deep South freaks me out at night. It's all those stories about swamps, crocodiles, and toothless guys with shotguns running around. And if that's not bad enough, when you drive through Louisiana, the highway goes up over the Atchafalaya Swamp for eighteen miles! If that's not the stuff of nightmares, I don't know what is.

One evening coming into Houston from the east it's that time between dusk and dark. The sun is gone, it's not quite dark, and your eyes are straining. There's some traffic and I've just come through a bunch of construction, so the lanes are really narrow.

I'm keeping up with traffic going a little faster than I ordinarily do. I'm listening to Dylan's *Blood On The Tracks*. *Shelter From The Storm* is playing and I'm thinking about an old love. The road does that to you. You replay things you said and mistakes you made years earlier, knowing that no amount of re-thinking would've changed anything. But you replay it anyway.

Out of the corner of my eye I see a figure. It's a man and he's leaping over the highway divider. He's heading straight for my front fender! I can't swerve because there are cars everywhere.

In a split second I see him freeze right before he steps in front of me. I'm shocked that my mirror doesn't hit him as I pass. I'm putting on my brakes, trying to slow down but not stop. It would be a chain-reaction disaster if I stop. I still don't know how I missed him.

I glance at my rearview mirror and see him dart across my lane behind me. He pauses and then crosses the next lane, after that I lose him. I'm hyperventilating I'm so scared.

I pull off at the next exit to get gas. Even though I don't need any.

RANDOM SNAPSHOTS

At a rest stop in Indiana, I look west. Huge menacing black clouds are heading our way.

I approach a truck driver in the parking lot.

"Excuse me. Do you know anything about that storm?" I point at the clouds.

"It's bad. Visibility's zero. We're all staying here till it passes."

"Any idea how long it'll last?"

"From what I'm hearing, it'll be here in about twenty minutes and it'll last about forty-five. You don't want to be out there if you don't need to."

I go back to the van, make myself a sandwich, give Moses a biscuit, sit back and wait for the storm to blow through. And, boy, does it.

It rains so hard I can't see anything out my windshield and

the wind is rocking the van like crazy. Moses looks at me with one of those, "Why are we doing this again?" expressions. I pet him. Sometimes it's very calming and reassuring to have your dog right there with you.

Once the storm blows through I follow the trucks out on to the highway.

So many people complain about truck drivers: They're rude, the trucks are too big, or they drive badly. I disagree.

Maybe it's because I've driven so many miles over the years but I've found that most truck drivers are good people who are just trying to earn a living. When I'm lost or have questions about the roads or the weather, I ask truck drivers and most of them are a great help.

A couple days later we're driving though a lesser storm that's still pretty intense. I pull into a rest area for a break.

I open up the back of the van to get something out of the cooler when I hear a voice behind me.

"Excuse me."

I jump and almost hit my head on the open tailgate. I spin around and there's a trucker, a good six-foot-three, maybe fifty years old.

"I'm sorry, I didn't mean to scare you."

"No problem. Just lost in thought. What do you need?"

"You passed me a few miles down the road and I noticed that one of your roof boxes was loose. The front end was coming up like it wasn't closed properly. I thought you should check it."

I walk to the passenger side and look up at the box that would have been on his side when I passed. Sure enough the front end is partially open.

One good burst of wind could have torn the top off it and dumped merchandise and clothes all over the highway. It also could have caused an accident.

"Wow. Thanks."

"You're welcome. Drive safe."

I now check both roof boxes every day.

FINDING NEMO

At a film festival I wander into the vendor area hoping for free food and booze. If you want film people to show up to your event just tell them there's free food and booze.

This is the place where all the gear nerds get hard-ons. It's all the newest gear and software for filmmaking. While they're talking techno-speak with the company reps, I'm looking to see who's got the best snacks. I never get hung up on gear at these places. One, I can't afford it; and two, I'm more concerned about telling good stories than doing cool shit with the latest gear.

There's a quote from Terry Gilliam that I've always loved. It is something along the lines of, if you want to be a filmmaker, don't go to film school. You need to learn about art, architecture, literature, philosophy, history, and so many other things so that your films are about something! You can always learn about equipment later.

Even though I went to film school, I think of this quote every time I see a gathering of film nerds and all they want to talk about is gear.

As I walk past one vendor, I see this skinny Asian guy with the longest dread locks I've ever seen on anyone! I *gotta* stop.

"I don't know who you are or what you're selling, but I had to come over."

"Never seen an Asian kid with dreadlocks before?"

"Can't say that I have."

"Nemo." He stuck out his hand.

"Kelley Baker, also known as the Angry Filmmaker."

"Angry Filmmaker, now that's a story I gotta hear."

"You first."

Needless to say we hit it off and talk for quite awhile. Nemo is hilarious and jam-packed with energy. I find out later he plays drums, probably to channel some of that energy. And there's no better use of energy than hitting stuff.

We exchange cards and keep in touch. Nemo arranges a booking for me at his alma mater. He gets them to pony up more money than I would have charged them. Now that's a friend.

He's always calling and emailing me with ideas on how to build my audience and how to market myself better than I do. He's quite a guy. And I've still never seen another Asian kid with dreadlocks. Especially as long as his.

LOOK AT THE SIZE OF THOSE HANDS

I don't care what anyone says, I'm not feeling any closer to God at this moment.

I'm standing with Jeff and Amber in the Prayer Tower at Oral Roberts University looking out over Tulsa. Part of Tulsa, anyway.

Moments before this we had been wandering around the campus and I was amazed at how clean cut everyone was. Young women in dresses, young men in white shirts and ties. It's kind of creepy. These people are too wholesome for my tastes and even though it's obvious we don't belong here, they are unfailingly polite. Which bothers me even more.

The campus is beautiful and overly manicured. I'm not surprised it's run by a TV evangelist – not a blade of grass out of place, just like his hair. The upkeep on this place must be expensive, not that it matters. These people don't pay for it anyway.

"We are asking you good people for more donations to help us get the word out about God and to cover our overhead. So call us today. Praise Jesus! Amen!"

I'm convinced there are cameras watching our every move and these clean-cut robots, I mean kids, are being sent out to make sure we don't do something disrespectful. Whatever that might be?

Yes, the giant praying hands at the entrance are very impressive, but they're nothing compared to the Prayer Tower.

The Prayer Tower is where Oral goes to pray to God to get

his followers to send him more cash. I remember one time he was saying something about if he couldn't raise a certain amount of money in a few days that God was going to call him home. Which sounds to me like God is going to kill him if he fails. Somehow the way he says that makes God sound like a loan shark and if Oral doesn't come up with the money then He is going to ice him. Which is an interesting perspective.

I know Oral isn't running the place day-to-day anymore. Like any good family business, it's now being run by the next generation, his son Richard (although Richard and family are eventually deposed in a bloodless coup over their outrageous spending habits, but this is still in the future.)

It's very quiet in the tower, like a library or a morgue. I can see why Oral would want to come up here to meditate, pray, play solitaire, or whatever it is he really does while he's waiting for the cash to come pouring in. I wander around taking it all in. There are other people here who are obviously more in awe of the place than I am.

Suddenly it hits me and, unfortunately, I blurt it out to my friends.

"Do you realize that this whole place is run by two guys named Oral and Dick?"

Jeff and Amber's eyes go wide and they look around quickly to see if anyone else has heard me. They have.

Judging by the looks we're getting, it's time to go. Now, I can't prove it, but I'm absolutely convinced we're followed all the way to the parking lot and our license plate is probably written down somewhere in their security files.

Needless to say, I haven't been back.

A NORTHERNER WALKS INTO A BAR...

In Memphis after a screening, some friends take me to what's supposed to be one of Memphis' oldest bars, Earnestine & Hazels' Bar & Grill.

The place hasn't been updated or gentrified. It used to be a brothel, and you can feel the ghosts. It's my kind of bar. The downstairs is noisy so we head upstairs where there's a smaller bar and lots of deserted rooms. The hallways are dark and the empty rooms we pass have either a single dim light on or they're dark. It takes some time for my eyes to get used to the place. Most of the walls are brick and the hallway floor is all wood. It squeaks as we walk. I'm sure there are a lot of stories in this place.

There are three empty stools at the bar. I'm introduced to the longtime bartender and off we go. I'm always up for interesting stories and the bartender regales us with tales of the past. He's probably told these stories a hundred times but he's a natural storyteller and he brings this place and it's past to life. I'm enthralled.

On my right is a young woman, probably late twenties, sitting by herself. I foolishly think if she's interested why not include her in the conversation?

I ask a simple question and she turns on me.

"I don't talk to anyone who's from north of the Mason-Dixon line!"

Her eyes burn with hatred. Where did that come from?

"Excuse me?"

"You heard me."

Oh, I did. And for the life of me I can't let it go.

"You got me. I'm from the North, alright. In fact my family is from Northern Scotland. So while you guys were over here having your little war with each other, we were fighting the British, for hundreds of years! Hell, my family didn't even come here until the 1920s and that was by way of Canada. Glad to know you have such an open mind when it comes to geography. I'm not sure how you sleep at night, but my guess is it's alone."

I turn away from her and back to my friends who, having witnessed this outburst, are staring at me. Now, I know I was being a prick by saying that last line, but I couldn't help it. Some people just bring out the best in me.

I'm not sure how long she stayed because I never looked back in her direction. She sure had a belly full of hate for people from the North, and I find that sad. The war is over, lady, and like most wars, nobody won.

MOM AND POP VIDEO STORES

Everywhere I go I ask people if they know of any independent video stores, places where I might sell a few DVDs.

I hear about this hard-core independent video store run by a couple of heavy metal guys who love movies and tattoos. It's in an old run down house in kind of a rough neighborhood. Inside feels like one-part video store and one-part party house. DVDs are scattered everywhere but they're all in order. It's organized chaos which makes me feel very comfortable. The two guys that work here are big, pierced, and heavily tattooed wearing old black T-shirts with faded band names across the front.

I introduce myself, tell them what I'm doing, and ask if they'd be interested in buying any of my DVDs, as I can use the money, being on the road and all.

"Whatta ya got?"

"Three features, a short film compilation, and a one-hour doc."

"Whatta ya want for 'em?"

"Ten dollars each?"

"Take cash?"

"If you have cash I'll give you all five for forty."

"Nah. We'll pay cash and give ya fifty. What you're doing is cool. I always wanted to tour the country with my dog."

I stop at small independent video stores all over the country and it's always the same. Ninety percent of the time they buy something without watching it or knowing who I am. The people who run these stores are no different than people who run independent bookstores. They do it for love because you know damn well they aren't making much money.

One of my favorites in Madison, Wisconsin, had a T-shirt they sold that said, "Where Fellini's 8 1/2 is always in stock." I ended up swapping my DVDs for one of their shirts. I gave it to Fiona when I got home.

It's a shame most of these places are gone now.

DOGS, POLITICS, MOONSHINE and LIFE
(ERIC and MISS MELANIE)

Outside a Motel 6, Moses is stretching his legs and leaving his mark on a bush when a raised four-wheel drive pick-up pulls into the parking lot. Out gets this burly looking character with a shaved head and a goatee. This guy is muscular and he moves with confidence. He looks like your typical redneck and he heads straight for Moses and I.

Shit, I don't need any hassles from some local dude.

"Pardon me sir. Would it be alright if I pet your dog?"

"Excuse me?"

"Would it be alright if I pet your dog. I love Labs."

"By all means."

This guy gets down on his knees and starts petting Moses. He has a big smile on his face and when he scratches Moses right above his tail he has a friend for life. There is something about a dog that brings out the best in people.

The van is still under warranty, barely, and I need to take advantage of the last free check up. I decide to get all of the maintenance done since I have a couple days off. The dealer in Franklin, Tennessee, says they can do everything the following day. I find a decent motel for a couple days so I can rest. My needs are simple: a clean place with a good shower and a comfortable bed that contains no other living creatures.

I consider myself something of an expert on motels, which is why my preference is Motel 6. They're pretty inexpensive, there are a lot of them, and they all take dogs.

Disclaimer: I've stayed in a lot of Motel 6s and I'm not on their payroll, nor have I ever seen Tom Bodett in one. He's probably left after leaving the light on for me.

"You staying here?"

"Just a couple nights. I gotta get some work done on my van."

"I've been here a week. Looking for a house in the area for me and my wife. I'm Eric."

"Kelley."

"I've always had Labs, I love 'em. You know, if a man is lucky he will have two great dogs in his life. I've had three and I feel truly blessed."

This is one of the nicest things I've ever heard anyone say about dogs. And you know what? I've had four dogs and they were all great. All of a sudden I'm feeling pretty blessed, too.

Eric enjoys talking and soon he's telling me all about himself.

This is his second trip to the area. Last time he stayed here for two weeks. His wife's coming up tomorrow and they'll be checking out a few houses that he's already seen.

He suggests grabbing dinner at a local restaurant.

"Sure, after five weeks on the road it'd be nice to have some company."

I tell him I'm a filmmaker and ask if I can shoot a short conversation with him. "It's something I like to do when I meet interesting people on the road. I want to talk about the American Dream."

He gets flustered, says he doesn't have much to say that anyone would find interesting, but finally agrees.

When I get up to his room, I see that he's changed into a nice dress shirt. I don't say anything. He starts out a little nervous but after a bit he relaxes and we have a nice conversation. He suggests a drink before dinner as he has a bottle of whiskey and some ice.

I knew I liked this guy.

We knock back a drink and off to the restaurant we go.

My initial impression of Eric is totally wrong. He's the kind of guy who takes people at face value. I'm sure he figures I'm a good guy because I own a Lab.

We drink wine and laugh our way through dinner. Our waitress keeps checking on us because we've become her favorite customers. We talk about a lot of things, even politics. It's obvious we don't agree on a lot of things, but that doesn't slow down the conversation. Eric's a man who listens, thinks about what you say, and replies. Between us there's mutual respect for each other and each other's opinions.

Eric comes from the Delta and likes to stay busy. Since retiring he's had quite a few different jobs. And with every job he's got a good story or two. He refers to his wife as "Miss Melanie." She's retiring soon and he's going to manage a hunting area for a group of business people here in Franklin.

Apparently business people who like to hunt will buy hundreds of undeveloped acres and hire someone to manage it. Eric loves the outdoors and knows the types of plants to grow in certain areas that attract whatever type of game the place is going to specialize in.

He wants me to meet Miss Melanie and suggests the three of us have dinner the following night.

At five-thirty the next evening, I meet Eric and Miss Melanie in the lobby and we end up back at the same restaurant. Eric and I take up where we left off the previous night. Finally Miss Melanie looks at me and says, "You two act like you've known each other for years!"

I take that as a compliment.

Eric and I keep in touch and the following year I'm going to be passing through Franklin again. I send him a note and ask if he's going to be around, maybe we can grab a meal?

He and Miss Melanie insist that Moses and I stay with them.

Looking at my calendar I see that I'll be staying there around the same time of the Father-Daughter Dance back in Portland. I decide to ask Eric if he can watch Moses for the thirty hours I'll be in Portland. I give him a call.

"Hey man, I need a favor and I feel funny asking, but I am hoping you can help me out."

"If I can."

"I have to fly to Portland to attend Fiona's father-daughter dance around the time I'm staying with you. I'm wondering, and if it's a hassle feel free to say no, but I'm wondering if you could watch Moses for the two days I'll be gone."

There's a long silence on the phone. I'm starting to wonder if I've insulted him or pissed him off or something.

"Brother, I'd be honored to watch Moses for you."

"Really?"

"I know what that dog means to you and I know what my dogs mean to me. I wouldn't want just anyone to watch them while I was gone. I am honored and humbled that you think enough of me to watch him. Of course I will and I'll take real good care of him, too."

"I know you will."

"Thank you for asking, brother."

I arrive two weeks later. It's hot and humid when I arrive but Eric's ready for me. He's packed a cooler with beers and some water out on the front porch. I finally get to meet his old hunting dog, a big black Lab named Billy. He moves slowly and painfully but follows Eric everywhere. He and this dog are tight.

The two of them haven't gone hunting in a long time as Billy has bad arthritis. Some of Eric's friends wondered why he hasn't put the dog down since he's so old and not moving well. "As long as old Billy still wants to get around and wag his tail, then I'm gonna take care of him to the best of my ability."

Moses and Billy get along quite well. Moses has respect for his elders.

We sit on the front porch in rocking chairs drinking ice-cold beer and talking about what we've been doing for the last year.

Before dinner Eric asks if I'd like a cocktail, even though we've been drinking beer all afternoon. John Steinbeck always offered visitors a cup of coffee and occasionally he would "add a little to it," which is definitely old school. I know I'm remiss in not carrying a bottle of whiskey in the van, but there you are.

A glass of whiskey with a touch of ice sounds good. As we're sipping our whiskey the subject of moonshine comes up. I confess that I've never had any. I'm sure there are people making it out in the Pacific Northwest but I don't know any of them. Besides, moonshine just seems like a Southern thing to me.

Eric is appalled. Immediately I'm standing in front of a spare refrigerator that has a few Mason jars in it.

"I get this from a good ol' boy in Missouri. He cuts it with just a little bit of apple."

He opens a jar and hands it to me. A true Southern gentleman.

I take just a sip because I'm a little nervous. That shit is strong! And it's pretty good! Eric has a drink and hands it back to me. I take a bigger swig and feel the warmth go all the way down my throat and into my stomach.

"Man, I'll bet drinking enough of this stuff could really do some damage."

Eric winks and smiles. "Brother, you don't know half."

It's at this moment we both realize that we've been drinking beer all day, switched to whiskey, and we're now imbibing moonshine. And we haven't had dinner yet.

Eric puts the jar away. Good idea.

"Miss Melanie is making chicken and dumplings just for you. She doesn't do it all that often and it's a real favorite."

Now, I've had chicken and dumplings before, and honestly I'm not a fan. It's a bunch of dough tossed into some watery gravy, usually pretty bland. Coming from the Northwest, some foods just don't translate well. I've had chicken and dumplings in some good restaurants and have been less than impressed. Friends have made them and I politely ate them, but I wouldn't go out of my way to have them again.

Then I had Miss Melanie's chicken and dumplings. The dumplings were so soft, the gravy so flavorful, and the chicken amazingly tender. It blew my mind.

Eric says she always makes hers with lots of love. Oh yeah. Now I get it.

The next day Eric takes Moses and me up to the hunting area. It's wild forestland with dirt roads that run through it. It's gorgeous and quiet. I see why Eric likes it up here. He's always on the lookout for people trespassing or camping because it's private property. It makes him nervous when he finds someone.

"You never know who you might run into and they're probably armed. I just don't want any trouble, you know?"

I know. Up on the ridges the views are spectacular. You can see for miles. It's pretty humid so we stop at a small lake and let Moses cool off. Like a good Lab he leaps right in.

This trip gives me a little view into Eric's life. He's worked hard to get here but it's obvious the outdoors agrees with him.

I fly to Portland the following day. Fiona and I have a great time at the dance and then I fly back to Tennessee. I arrive at Eric's house to find the most content dog in the world. Moses is happy to see me but I can tell he's been spoiled rotten while I've been gone.

"I hope he's been okay. Hasn't caused any trouble."

"He's been the perfect gentleman."

Southern hospitality, when it's genuine, is something special.

A month later I'm stuck in traffic trying to get out of Southern California when I get a call from Eric.

"You okay, brother?"

"Fine man, what's going on?"

"We've been watching the TV and seeing that Oregon and Washington are getting all sorts of bad weather. We wanted to make sure you and Moses are okay."

"We're still in Southern California. I've been talking to my folks and they say the weather isn't as bad as what's on the news."

"Miss Melanie and I've been worried about you two."

"You tell Miss Melanie not to worry, Moses and I are okay. Besides we're from there. We're used to the weather."

"Well you drive safe, brother."

"I will, my friend. I will."

I run into Eric one more time, on TV.

It's during the presidential campaign of 2008 and I'm in Minneapolis doing some workshops for a friend. After dinner his wife says, "Let's watch the second debate."

The second presidential debate is taking place at Belmont University in Nashville. It's the only debate that's being done as a town-hall style meeting. Members of the audience get to ask questions of the candidates.

I'm sitting there with a glass of wine in my hand when Tom Brokaw introduces the first person with a question.

"Oh my God! That's Eric!" I almost spill my wine.

"Who's Eric?"

"We were drinking moonshine just a few months ago."

"What?"

"I'll explain later."

Eric's all dressed up in a suit, he's wearing glasses, and I'll be damned if he hasn't shaved his goatee off. I wouldn't have recognized him, until I heard his voice.

I send him an email later that went something like this:

"Just saw you on TV at the debates. Boy, did the Secret Service screw up or what? Letting a guy like you close to the presidential candidates. I fear for the security of our nation.

Nothing personal.
Please give my best to Miss Melanie."

As I recall his reply went, "Yeah, I'll say somebody screwed up. It was quite the experience though and I'm hearing from a lot of people. Hope you and Moses are well. When you coming back this way, brother?"

I still need to do that.

SKINNY PEOPLE FLY. FAT PEOPLE DRIVE.

When I was a kid we traveled by car. My father always said, "Go where the truck drivers eat, they know good food." I'm sure some of them know good food, but what they really know is where to get a lot of food, cheap.

Now I'm not a small person. Sure I'm smaller than Kevin Smith but I'm larger than Spielberg. I stand five feet ten inches tall and my weight fluctuates between two hundred and two hundred twenty pounds. I've been battling my weight for years.

I'm also an asthmatic. I was at my pulmonologist's office for a check up a while back and I saw all of these people on oxygen. They were overweight, had trouble walking around, and they had to drag their portable oxygen tanks with them. My biggest fear is that's my future. I'm also aware that a lot of those folks smoked and except for one brief week in high school I was never a fan of cigarettes.

I had a long talk with my doctor who told me that I had a choice. I can keep walking, watch what I eat, and stay active. Or I can become sedentary and help put his kids through college. I continue to work on the former.

In January of 2013 I had two open-heart surgeries. I had a double bypass and a new aortic valve installed. (They also changed the oil and added a new filter.) So that certainly colors the way I look at things now. But even before then I had these same thoughts.

On the road, it's disturbing how unhealthy people look, and how much trouble some of them have just walking to the restroom from the parking lot. I see lots of canes, walkers, and out of breath sweaty people, who are younger than I am. I understand that some people have health issues and they're overweight because of those issues.

I've seen more heavy truck drivers than I have fat pilots. And let's face it, sitting behind the wheel for hours on end is not really conducive to a good cardiovascular workout. Pilots on the other hand do sit in the cockpit for hours but they also have to navigate different airports and getting to gates just like the rest of us. And they are pulling their bags with them. As a frequent passenger I know that anytime spent in an airport can be quite the cardio workout.

Truckers drive for hours and hours and most get paid by the

mile. The more they stop the fewer miles they drive, which usually means less money in their pockets. Most of the road restaurants are fast-food chains and they do have "healthy" things on their menus like salads. But, once you add salad dressing and other toppings, the myth that salads are good for you disintegrates.

And this isn't just about truck drivers. This is about a culture: the culture of the road trip. In a car the drive is a large part of the journey. When you fly it's about the destination.

For most people, road trips are a time to eat junk food and drink sixty-four ounce sodas. "It's a vacation, we're having fun." And when you walk into truck stops or convenience stores on the road, the first things you see are candy, pastries and caffeine in some form or another. Of course the owners of these places do this on purpose. They know this stuff is hard to pass up.

I'm not saying I don't want to eat junk food. Of course I do. All of that sugar and deep fried stuff is something that I enjoy like everyone else. But I know what that stuff does to me when I eat it. I get lethargic. I want to take a nap. I also get hungrier faster than I normally would because my body is crying out for more of that crap.

And a lot of people who are overweight avoid flying, as they don't want the embarrassment of having to buy an extra seat. We're all vain, we all have egos. I certainly do and, if I had to buy an extra seat on a plane, I probably wouldn't fly much either.

I get it. Diet is a choice. Healthy eating is a choice.

We need to do something about our national diet. It's wrong that so many people have health problems because of diet. It bothers me that so many people have problems getting in and out of cars. On the road I see them with young children and I worry that they can't be active with their kids. They may not live to see their kids grow up and have kids and they're not having the quality of life that they should.

I think about this every time I'm on the road.

I think geography has something to do with it as well. As I've written, in the South so many things are fried. Now maybe not more than other places, but it feels that way. In the Midwest there are a lot of meat-and-potato places. And no matter where you go, you're served giant portions. In fact, we feel like we've been ripped off if we don't get huge portions.

It's against our principles to throw food out. My parents grew up during the Depression when food (and money) was scarce. I remember being told to clean my plate because there were starving children in "Red China."

On the road, I used to find myself eating more than I intend to because I can't take it with me. Even though I have a cooler, most restaurant food doesn't preserve well in there. And even if it preserves okay it looks pretty scary the next day with things coagulating.

I also fall into the "I've had a rough day, lots of driving in shitty weather, a small turnout at my gig, no one laughed at my jokes, I should have sold more merch," so I deserve this all-you-can-eat Chinese buffet.

And I can say for a fact that even Moses eats more doggie junk food on the road than he does when we're home. I always throw him a couple biscuits when we stop, when we check into a motel, and certainly when we go to bed at night. But they are always dog treats. It wasn't until Moses got old that I would give him the occasional piece of cheese. I've always believed that you don't give dog's human food for two reasons: I don't think it's good for them, and when you have a dog the size of Moses, what you don't want to create is a one-hundred-twenty-pound beggar.

It took time, but for the most part I don't overeat on the road. I have a tough time sleeping if my stomach is stuffed with food. And if I do sleep, I don't sleep well. Combine that with driving hundreds of miles a day and no time for naps and now I do eat pretty moderately.

I'm overweight enough that I know that some of the things I've had the opportunity to do on the road would have been much easier if I was lighter. I will always struggle with my weight and my goal as always is to eat as healthy as possible. There are too many things I want to do.

THE LENGTHS I WILL GO

It's dark. Too dark. What the hell am I doing awake? What time is it?

I grope around feeling for my phone. It must have fallen off the couch last night. I reach down trying to find it on the carpeted floor without getting up. It's freezing and I don't want to get up any earlier than I have to.

I'm halfway off the couch when I finally find it. Four-twenty-eight a.m. I woke up just before the alarm goes off. Figures.

I want to roll over and go back to sleep but that's not happening. I've been looking forward to this day for months. I get up, throw some clothes on, and turn on a small light. I'm sleeping in the basement so I won't wake anyone up as I move around.

Moses and I sneak out the door just before five a.m., trying to be as quiet as possible. Which is a challenge since I'm carrying a bag of clothes and Moses' bed, and I have Moses on his leash. I feel like I'm running out on a bill, like I owe money to someone. I'm fumbling with the van keys as I look around and make sure I've got everything. The front door locks behind me. If I've forgotten anything, it's too late now.

I repacked the van last night so all we have to do is get in and go. That is, after Moses sniffs around and does his last bit of marking. I'm dying for coffee.

What the hell's going on?

I'm on my way to a Dada and Surrealist exhibition that's only making one stop in the United States. Cincinnati? Really? Somehow this makes sense in a Dada and Surreal way.

I'm a huge fan of both the Dada and Surrealist movements and when I saw the pieces that are in the exhibition I have to be there. This is probably my only chance to see these pieces as they're from a museum in Israel and they rarely travel.

I arrange my tour so I can be near Cincinnati. I have a two-day gap between bookings. It doesn't work out as I'd planned and I'm not as close as I want to be. I have to drive to Cincinnati in one day and get there early enough, so I can see the exhibit before the museum closes. It's Sunday and the museum's closed on Mondays. This is my only window.

I'm in eastern Pennsylvania and, since it's a Sunday morning, it's just the semis and us on the highway. The drive takes almost ten hours and is uneventful. No accidents and no traffic jams.

I'm fried as I pull into the museum parking lot at three p.m., but I'm also excited. I'm getting a second wind. I have three hours to see the exhibit. I park under a tree and leave the side windows open so Moses stays cool.

The exhibit is well worth the drive. There are pieces by Marcel Duchamp, Max Ernst, Salvador Dali, Hannah Hoch, Rene Magritte and Paul Delvaux, among others. I once took a train from London to Brussels and stayed there two days just to see a major Magritte retrospective, I'm that fanatical about the Surrealists. I still have the catalog at home.

Some pieces I've seen photos of, others I've never heard of, let alone seen. It's amazing. I wander through the entire exhibit twice. I read, I look, I study, I relax, and I enjoy.

The exhibition is busy, but not crowded. It's easy to move among the pieces and I never feel like I'm in anyone's way. I get some strange looks from a few of the guards as I am checking out some pieces multiple times. Their looks probably have more to do with the fact that I have just driven ten hours on only a few hours sleep and I'm sure I look just this side of deranged.

I don't care. I stay until the museum closes. I walk out feeling energized. This is what great art does to me. It makes me happy. I'm no longer tired from the drive.

I let Moses out of the van and we find a nice piece of grass with a table. We dine al fresco. There's a wonderful view where we sit, and no one bothers us. It's one of my favorite days on the road. I'm inspired and I feel great.

WHAT STRANGE HELL is THIS?

I hit the floor with a thud.

"Watch his shoulder, watch his shoulder!" Professor Danger yells.

The Death Falcon immediately backs off.

"Did I hurt ya, man?"

"I'm okay," I say through clenched teeth.

"What's with your shoulder?"

"Tore the rotator cuff years ago hauling heavy film equipment up three flights of stairs in Paris. No insurance so it's never been fixed. Every now and then it hurts like a motherfucker."

I stagger to my feet and try to brush it off.

"You shoulda said something, man. I don't want to hurt ya."

"I thought that was the point."

"That's never the point. Professional wrestling is not fake! The outcome is always decided before you enter the ring.

So you have to sell the audience on the storyline. It has to look real."

It certainly feels real to me right now.

I'm standing in a wrestling ring set up in an old brick school somewhere in West Virginia. The ring barely fits inside this room. There are a couple folding chairs strewn about and you can barely walk around the outside of the ring. Off to one side is an old janitor's closet complete with giant ceramic sink that can easily hold one of those old metal buckets on wheels that many a janitor pushed around the hallways with a giant stringy mop inside.

Cue Rod Serling. I know he's hiding around here somewhere. I'm positive I've stepped back into the early 1960s and someone has stuffed this full-sized wrestling ring into this tiny room.

The reason I'm in town is to speak at WVSU. I'm staying with my buddy, Professor Danger, also known as Danny – a filmmaker, professor, author, Fulbright recipient, mountain climber, bull rider, and professional wrestler. A Renaissance man.

Danny and I met many tours ago. I try to see him on every tour. Whether I lecture or not, I need to sit in a dimly lit neighborhood bar with Danny knocking back Yuenglings and catching up. It's cathartic. Sharing stories about our past, how far we've come, and where we may or may not be headed.

I foolishly ask about professional wrestling and the next thing I know I'm squared off in the ring with the Death Falcon. I think I'm the practice dummy. (Remind me never to ask about bull riding.)

He shows me a few moves and then it begins. I'm amazed how fast he is and how quickly I'm getting knocked around. I'm pissed at myself. I'm not putting up as much of a fight as I thought I would. All that time and experience on the playgrounds of my youth are not helping me. I know I'm not much of a bad ass but I'm not even making it difficult. There goes any dream of being Hemingway, or even Plimpton.

Danny is shooting with my camera and he and the Death Falcon are explaining things to me as we're moving around the ring.

Before I know it I'm in a headlock. Then I'm on the ground, pinned.

At six-foot-four and a rock solid two-hundred-forty pounds, the Death Falcon (his real name is Bill) is a lot bigger, stronger and faster than I am. He's also a few hours shy of his master's degree in English literature and the author of several books of short stories.

On a break I ask, "You're an intelligent fellow, and an author. Why wrestling?"

He smiles a scary smile. "I went through a really bad divorce a while back and I really wanted to hit something! And you know I can do this legally…" His voice trails off.

I have to admit this type of wrestling is a lot harder than I thought it would be, but I come through it relatively unscathed. I grab Moses out of the van and we all grab lunch.

Danny and I are the same age. I'll politely say in our 50s.

He's not a physically imposing fellow, or macho in the way you think of traditional wrestlers. Then again, neither is Bill. They're very calm and low key. They also won't back down when they're pushed.

"You are an educated guy. You've received a couple of Fulbright Scholarships and helped set up a filmmaking program at a sister school in Africa. Why wrestling?" I ask Danny.

"It's storytelling in a different way. It's part theater because things change for every performance. And like a play, once a performance is done, that's it. There's no editing. It all exists for one night, one performance."

Danny and Bill teach me enough about professional wrestling and wrestlers that I'm sure it's not something I can fall back on if filmmaking and writing don't work out.

They wrestle because they enjoy it. Like theater and film they have learned the art of making fights look real, but for the most part they're choreographed so that nobody really gets hurt.

That doesn't mean they don't get hurt. Sometimes it happens. And no matter how careful they are, there are a lot of bruises, scars, sore muscles and some broken bones, as well as concussions that occur in the ring. Or right outside of it. There is an art to getting hit with a folding chair or being thrown on to a collapsing table and being able to get back up and continue. And there is no director yelling, "Cut!" after a fall.

Most of the guys are professionals and try not to hurt each

other. But like any profession there are some assholes that don't play well with others. They believe their future is the big time and they take their own self-importance a little too seriously. There can be bad blood between some of these guys, especially if they do things that are not considered right by the veterans in the ring.

Things can get out of hand and then shit gets real.

Sometimes the scariest part is the audience in some small towns. I'm told they really get into it and if you're the designated bad guy in a match, expect no mercy from the crowd. The smart wrestlers know how to work a crowd. People are screaming at you. They're taking their frustrations out. I think it would still be advisable to leave the venue in a group.

I have so much respect for these guys. I really do see what they do as an art form, just like the theater.

Bill tells me that some of the "older wrestlers" are also avid readers and that I wouldn't believe some of the literary discussions he's had between matches. Somehow I can't image these big beefy guys discussing the classics, but I also know Bill and if he says it, then it happens. But their fans?

WELCOME TO HELL, YOUR TABLE IS READY

Moses and I are passing through West Virginia. I have no gigs but Danny says come by. We arrive and he's in a hurry. We have to pick up Bill. There's a big wrestling event and we have to be there.

What's this wrestling thing? Are he and Bill wrestling? Should I grab my camera? Why the big hurry?

We pick up Bill and I find out. One of those big wrestling events is on pay-per-view and we're headed to Hooters to meet up with some other wrestlers to watch it.

Wait a minute? We're going to Hooters? I confess that I've never been to Hooters. I have my own images, but I ask Bill what it's like in there.

"You've seen those Hooters billboards with those beautiful girls on them?"

"Yeah."

"Well, none of them work where we're going."

By the time we get to Hooters, it's packed. The guy at the door says they're too full. Can't let us in. No tables available.

Danny asks, "If I can find us a table would you let us in?"

"Sure but there's no way..."

Danny's back in about ten seconds. "Those two guys over there said we could share their table."

I look over and see two extremely obese kids in white t-shirts and baggy shorts slamming deep-fried food and drinking giant sodas. And I mean the fifty-five gallon drum size. These guys look like they've been living in their parent's basements for years, rarely seeing the sun.

They smile at Danny and wave at the guy at the door.

"That's five bucks each!"

A five-dollar cover to sit in Hooters and watch wrestling? The guy's joking, right?

He wasn't. We paid.

I look around the place and realize, I'm in hell.

I don't want to sound like a horrible person but…oh, fuck it! I'm not a small dude, but I'm tiny next to most of the people in this place. Hell, even the waitress is bigger than me. And she could probably take me in a bare-knuckle brawl as well.

These two kids (they were in their late twenties) were really nice. They didn't have to share their table with us, but they did. It was then I realized: Danny and Bill were celebrities here. Minor celebrities that wouldn't show up on a Brat Pitt/Angelina Jolie scale, but celebrities all the same.

These kids are in heaven with us at their table. Actually they don't give a shit about me, I'm not a wrestler. Danny and Bill are so nice to these guys, talking to them, answering questions and really taking an interest in them. I just want to drink!

I take that back. I don't want to drink. I need to drink. What the hell am I doing here? The noise is deafening. There are TVs everywhere and people are screaming at them. Apparently everyone knows all the wrestlers and has opinions. What have I gotten myself into?

We order a large pitcher and I look at a menu. Everything in this place is deep-fried! Okay maybe it's not all deep-fried, but I'm not seeing a lot of healthy shit.

The waitress returns with our beer and pours three glasses. She leaves for a moment and then returns with a plastic bag full of ice.

"What's that for?"

"To keep the beer cold." she says as she drops the bag of ice INTO the pitcher!

Wait a minute? She just put a plastic bag into the beer. I don't know where that bag has been and even if it is clean, it's still a plastic bag in the beer! Is this some strange Hooters thing? What lame asshole thought of this? I can't wrap my head around this. There are fat people screaming at wrestlers on TV and I'm supposed to drink over-priced shitty beer with a plastic bag in it to keep it cold. Oh my God! What fresh hell can this be? (My apologies to Dorothy Parker.)

Bill sees my distress. He looks at the waitress. "Obviously you don't know who we are. We never let beer get warm. Then again it's Budweiser, the plastic might help the taste."

Truer words have never been spoken.

I pull the bag out of the pitcher and hand it back to her. We knock off the first pitcher in record time and go for a second. I'm forgoing food at this point. My arteries will thank me at a later date.

I'm spending more time watching the crowd than the matches. It is crazy here. The only time it calms down is between matches. Calming down is a relative term. The noise level never drops far and if people aren't yelling at the TV's they're yelling at each other. With each passing minute I feel like I'm descending farther and farther down into Dante's Inferno.

Pitcher number three arrives in the nick of time.

Bill starts quizzing me to draw my attention away from the crowd. Who's going to win each match? I guess them all correctly because it's classic story telling. It's obvious who the good guys are and who are the bad guys. The good guy is going to get the shit kicked out of him, look like he's about to be defeated, but like Charles Bronson or Clint Eastwood, it doesn't matter how beat up they get.

Good always triumphs. And the crowd goes crazy.

This isn't Shakespeare. Although some elements do remind me of…wait a fucking minute. I'm in Hooters with all of these crazy people screaming and yelling and I'm thinking about literature and story structure, when Danny leans in and says, "Remember, this is our audience." And he's right.

Is it getting hotter in here?

NATURE SCARES ME

We spend a week teaching in Nashville. Its sunny and humid one minute and pouring down rain the next. There are thunder and lightning storms off and on all week. I've been hearing about tornadoes and there are warnings posted. I'm teaching on the top floor and in the middle of one class it starts raining so hard that the students can't hear me.

I ask the students how we'll know if a tornado is heading our way. A student answers, "If you hear what sounds like a train coming at us, run. 'Cause there aren't any train tracks for miles."

After an intense week of teaching, my buddy William invites Moses and me up to the family farm. The farm's just outside of Nashville, a couple miles down a beat-to-hell dirt road in the middle of a forest. It's rustic as all hell and a great place to write.

One of those places that feels far away from everything and it's really quiet.

Until the sun goes down.

If you haven't experienced the bugs at night in the South, prepare yourself. There are thousands and they're incredibly loud. I'm amazed at how noisy nature can get. This house has screened-in porches. The evenings are warm and the bugs are everywhere. There is a lake with a small dam and a waterfall nearby and, even when the water is running fast, I can't hear it over the bugs.

Early each morning, Moses and I walk along the dirt road. I'm not sure if there are any trails in these woods and if there are, I'm not walking them alone. I've seen too many films about the woods that end badly.

Suddenly up a head we hear this weird noise. It's like nothing I've ever heard before. And it's not just a single sound, it's a bunch of sounds.

As we come around a bend, we see it. Walking toward us are ten wild turkeys. And they are huge! Moses tenses and I see the hair on his back go up. I get the leash on him quickly. I've heard that wild turkeys can be mean and aggressive. As big as Moses is, I'm not sure how we would fair against ten of these things. Moses doesn't bark. He just stands, watching. I'm not sure if any part of his gene pool kicks in at this moment, as he is a bird dog. I'm also not sure if he realizes that these monsters in front of us are actually birds.

The one in front watches us as it moves toward the trees, away from the road. The others follow. They continue making their strange calls. As they pass by, they all stare at us. The fur on Moses' back is still standing straight up, but he stays right next to me.

When we get back to the house I tell William and he says there's a lot of them out there but usually they stay away from the road. He's surprised they didn't sense Moses earlier and run for cover before we saw them.

It's getting hot. Moses and I decide to go for a swim in the lake. There's a small dock and as I'm taking my shoes off Moses walks to one side where there's a bunch of brush. He leans in and starts sniffing. Suddenly there's a huge splash, and it's not Moses. There's something in that brush that just jumped into the water, and it's not small. Moses jumps back and I jump a foot or two as well.

I'm looking at the water trying to see what just jumped in. I see the ripples of the initial splash and I keep waiting for something like the Loch Ness monster to surface. It doesn't.

I decide we don't need a swim after all. Moses loves swimming but it's obvious he agrees with me. We head back to the house.

I do not like nature.

ON the SUBJECT of DOGS and SWIMMING

It's hot. Damn hot. I'm sweating bullets. Us Northwest types don't do well with humidity. Never have. Never will. We're sitting in the backyard of Cari and Dave's house in Chicago. I met Cari when I spoke at Columbia College in Chicago but this is the first time I've stayed at their place. They have two dogs, one of which is very territorial. I suggested that the dogs meet on neutral territory so we took them on a short walk before we went to their house.

It didn't really matter because Shiva keeps growling at Moses and I keep asking if everything is okay?

Their fountain is on and, even though it's in the high eighties with matching humidity, the fountain makes it feel cooler. Okay, not really. But my workshops are done and we're enjoying a glass of wine. These are the nice, quiet moments during any tour where I don't have to be "on."

We're staring at the pond, which has all of these beautiful water lilies floating in it when Moses suddenly decides he's going for a swim. And like his namesake, when he leaps in to the pond he parts the sea. Water goes everywhere.

Oh shit! I really don't know these people and my dog just leaped in to their gorgeous pond. God only knows what kind of damage he's done! I look at Cari and Dave. What are they going to do?

Cari erupts in laughter and almost falls off her chair. "If you could see your face right now. You look horrified!" she says to me.

I look over at Moses who looks extremely content.

Cari and Dave assure me that sooner or later every dog that comes over always finds their way in to the pond. I am relieved. For a moment anyway.

The pond isn't very big, but it's deep and although he's cooled himself off, Moses now realizes that the sides of the pond are too steep and he can't get out. He isn't panicking yet, but he's not happy. Neither are the koi who are also in there.

Have you ever tried to lift a dripping wet hundred-and-twenty-pound dog out of a deep pond? There's no place to stand and get any leverage. He's also not keen on the idea of being pulled out.

With much pulling and personal discomfort, I'm able to get him out. Now I'm soaked. And although the water is cold, I'm not as refreshed as Moses is. But I'm happy to have provided so much laughter to Cari and Dave. Don't worry about me, I'll just sit in these wet clothes and have another glass of wine.

That's the funny thing about Moses. He's a water dog and if he sees water he's going in no matter where we are. I always keep a couple towels in the van and most of the time it works out fine, but every now and then he goes in somewhere he can't get out.

The worst is when he shoots down a really steep bank, leaps into a creek and, when he finally decides to get back out, he realizes that the bank is too steep and he can't climb back up. That's when I have to make my way down the slope and risk life and limb to get us both back up.

WE BOTH HATE DOG PARKS

Moses has never been a fan of other dogs. He harbors no ill will. He just doesn't like to hang out with them. He moves away when they get too close.

And since he's so big, most dogs want to fight him. They want to prove they're the local alpha. Then there are the small yapping dogs that have short-man (or small penis) syndrome.

Moses is a relaxed fellow and doesn't like to fight. I'm not saying he won't, he'd just prefer not to. I've seen him calmly walk away from aggressive dogs, both big and small. But when pushed he is a force of nature. And I have witnessed this.

There's always one dog that has to be the alpha and his or her owner is usually a dick. I have watched Moses move away while the other dog keeps coming at him. I've asked politely to get their dogs away from mine, pointing out that my dog doesn't wish to fight.

"Oh, he's just playing. That's how he plays. It's okay." Until Moses has had enough and snaps, usually sending the other dog flying backward.

Then I hear, "Your dog is dangerous! Your dog went after mine!" Or my favorite, "You need to learn how to control your dog!"

Moses comes walking back to me with his tail wagging as if he's just solved a problem and knows there won't be any others at this park.

THE DOG YELLER (I MEAN 'WHISPERER')

At one park we've frequented over the years, I've run into this guy who calls himself a dog "trainer." He's probably in his mid-sixties and he knows everything. You don't have to ask him, he always volunteers his knowledge. He'll say things like, "I used to train Labs, but not anymore. They'll break your heart." What the fuck does that mean? Or he'll say that Labs aren't obedient, they're stubborn. Whatever. Obviously he's not a fan of the breed.

He always has his young German shepherd on a long rope, one of those old braided ones. His dog always acts kind of strange when we run in to them. He never growls but when we see him his hackles are usually raised. Since he's on a leash (as is Moses) he never bothers us too much. As Moses and I walk around the park, I watch this guy giving commands but the dog never seems to pay much attention to him. I've never seen him strike the dog, but it's obvious his method isn't working.

One day as Moses and I are walking across the park from this yahoo I hear him yelling. At us. I look and his German shepherd has gotten off the rope and he's running straight for us. And he doesn't look like he wants to play.

I reach down and undo Moses' leash. I can see Mo's hackles are raised. I quietly say, "Go!"

Moses takes off running straight toward the German shepherd. He's moving a lot faster than I've ever seen him. He's like a freight train. The dogs get less than ten yards from each other when all of a sudden the shepherd slams on his brakes, tucks his tail between his legs, turns around, and starts heading back toward his owner as fast as he can.

Once Moses sees this he stops. Pauses. Then he turns around and comes walking back toward me like he's in no hurry.

"Good boy!" I put him back on his leash. Then I hear it. This guy is screaming at me! I hear, "Keep that dog on a leash! He's dangerous!" and on and on. I just stare at him.

Finally I give him the finger. Moses and I turn and continue our walk. I can still hear him yelling. We decide never to go back to that park again.

Eventually we stopped going to all dog parks. I still find places where I can let him off leash but away from people and other dogs.

With my AAA guidebooks we've found quite a few parks with lakes. If no one's around, I let him off the leash and he's swimming in no time.

At a lake in Texas I suddenly spot a large snake swimming.

I don't know what kind of snake it is, but it's probably not a good swimming companion. I call Mo and he comes right out. He is obedient.

EAST COAST DOG

Moses and I spend a few days relaxing on the outer banks of South Carolina. There's something really appealing about staying in a place called Kill Devil Hills. As usual, Moses is my emissary and introduces me to the locals.

He leaps out of the van and heads for people every chance he gets and this always starts conversations. The people at our motel love him and since he's with me I must be okay, too.

Here we learn about life in a place that depends on tourists and the tourist season. We're here a few weeks before the season starts and it's a sleepy little town where everyone's friendly. The locals tell me that, by the time fall rolls around, everyone is sick and tired of tourists but their bank accounts are replenished.

Our motel is right across the street from the Atlantic ocean. A couple times a day we cross the street and off he goes into the surf. While we're there some good-sized waves are breaking and he's having the time of his life. I walk along the beach and he keeps up with me, jumping in and out of the waves.

He may not be much of a retriever – he certainly doesn't fetch – but he is a one hundred percent water dog. He gets so much joy running in and out of the water and he always brings a smile to my face – until he gets too close and shakes off.

I like to think that when we do meet other dogs, Moses tells them about all the different places he's gone swimming: the Atlantic Ocean, two of the five Great Lakes and a bunch of small lakes and rivers all over the country. I also believe he loves the Pacific best, his home ocean. I'm sure to those other dogs Moses seems like a genuine explorer.

WHAT the HELL, IOWA?

I'm enjoying a beautiful sunrise and doing the speed limit because the van is fully loaded and I have out-of-state plates in forty-nine states. I'm not one to push my luck.

My morning coffee is doing its thing and I'm listening to the sound track from *Amadeus*. I'm at one with the universe this morning. I come around a nice, long, slow bend and there's an Iowa state trooper. He stares at me as I drive by.

I know immediately he's coming after me. I just have that gut feeling and my gut is rarely wrong.

Within moments, he's behind me, waiting for me to make a mistake. That's not going to happen because I've been driving for years and I'm pretty good at this. He sits behind me for a mile or two, then the lights come on.

I immediately pull over, turn off the car, roll down the

passenger window (I know from past experience that's where he's coming), and place both hands on the steering wheel so he can see them.

This guy is tall and skinny, probably shaves once a week at most. I'm not sure how long he's been driving a car, let alone being a cop. Isn't there some kind of minimum age you have to be before you can become a state trooper? God he looks wholesome.

"Where you headed?"

"Washington, D.C."

"What for?"

"I'm speaking at a film festival. Is there a problem?"

"The reason I pulled you over this morning is that your windows are too dark. They're illegal here in Iowa."

"Well, I'm not from Iowa. As you can see, I have Oregon plates and my windows are perfectly legal there."

"Can I see your license and registration?"

I slowly get my license out of my wallet, and the registration and my insurance card out of the glove box.

Why do the call it a glove box anyway? If I'm going to have gloves in the car I'd probably be wearing them or have them in my pocket or something. I wouldn't put them in a special box in the car. Anyway...

I pass these items through the window to him.

"Would you mind getting out of the van?"

He invites me to join him in his patrol car. I accept. Finally, a cop who isn't condescending and is actually polite.

As we sit in his car he runs down my license and registration. Sorry pal, no warrants.

He proceeds to tell me again about my illegally tinted windows.

"My van is registered in Oregon and the windows are legal there."

He doesn't say anything but I know he's thinking, "I got Jerry Garcia sitting in the car with me and I know there's drugs in that van…"

I'm not sure how I feel about the Jerry Garcia comparisons, but who knows, maybe in a few years they'll think I look like Willie Nelson. Which I guess is still better than people thinking I look like Kenny Rogers.

"If you want to look in the van to make sure I'm not hiding anything, feel free. But, so you know, I have a large, gentle dog in there on his bed on the passenger side and I'd appreciate it if you didn't let him out. We're too close to the road."

"What was the name of this film festival you say you're going to?"

"DC Shorts. I mean the DC Shorts Film Festival."

The guy actually looks it up on his computer.

"You're speaking there?"

"Yeah."

Wow this guy really doesn't believe me! I point to the link on the page that lists workshops and speakers and sure enough he follows the link and there's my picture.

"Wow. There you are."

Okay, I think, so now you know I'm who I say I am and I'm really going to the festival that starts in two days. Can I get out of here now?

"You know, I'm going to have to write up a warning about your windows."

"But I don't live in Iowa, the van is registered in Oregon where they are legal, and I'm literally just passing through. I don't understand why."

What I'm really thinking is, "You son of a bitch, you just wanted to pull me over and check me out. Now you have to justify this stop so you're writing up a warning that means nothing!"

But I continue to be polite.

He writes up his warning and hands it to me.

For some stupid reason I thank him as I get out of the patrol car. (Why did my parents raise me to always be so fucking polite?)

I file away the warning in the glove box and off I go, slowly.

So, the following year…

I'm driving that same stretch of road enjoying the sunrise. I come around the corner and there's an Iowa state trooper who checks me out as I pass. Once again he pulls out and follows me for about a mile before he turns his lights on.

Really?

Is this like some training place for rookies?

I shut off the van, roll down the passenger window, and keep my hands on the steering wheel. This guy is also really young looking. Unlike the guy from last year, he seems nervous.

"Can I see your license and registration, please?"

"Absolutely. The registration is in the glove compartment."

I slowly get my wallet out and pull out my license. I slowly open up the glove compartment and pull out the registration.

"Is there a problem?"

"The reason I stopped you is that your windows are too dark."

"They're perfectly legal in Oregon, and that's where I'm from."

"I see that. Would you mind stepping out of the car, sir?"

Once again I find myself in the passenger seat of his patrol car. I guess I should be grateful to be in the passenger seat and not handcuffed in the back.

We walk through the same stuff as we did last year even to the point of this guy going to the DC Shorts website and checking it out. (Thank you, Jon, for keeping your website updated.)

He also checks out my website. This is possibly the only time I wonder if having the "finger with sprocket holes running down it" as my logo is a good idea.

"I'm still gonna have to write you up a warning about those windows."

"Even though my car is not registered in Iowa and my windows are perfectly legal in Oregon?"

"These are our laws."

I want to tell this guy that every time I drive through Iowa I see cars with Iowa plates that have darker windows than I do. But I refrain.

I take my written warning and place it in the glove box next to last year's.

About ten miles down the road another Iowa state trooper pulls up behind me. I didn't see where he came from, but there he is.

What the hell?

He follows me for about a mile. Suddenly he pulls around me and takes off at high speed down the highway. Weird.

Thirty minutes later, I'm in Illinois and suddenly there's an Illinois state trooper behind me. He sits there for a couple miles. I can see he's watching me and he's on his radio.

What the hell is going on here? Have I stumbled into a Franz Kafka novel? My hands are shaking and I'm starting to freak out. And I haven't done anything! Am I under suspicion? Surveillance? Three troopers in thirty minutes? Maybe I don't look like Jerry Garcia. Maybe I look like Charles Manson!

Finally this guy pulls out and comes up next to me. He looks over at me and stays there for about fifteen seconds, studying me. I look back at him. Suddenly he waves, like everything is okay and takes off down the road.

I get off at the next exit, pull into a gas station parking lot and sit there shaking like a leaf for ten minutes. These cops have me totally unnerved. Is there some pervert driving a van that looks like mine? Or are these guys bored and just messing with me? Is it going to be like this all the way to D.C.?

I finally regain my composure and get the hell out of there. But I'm looking over my shoulder all the way through Illinois.

THIRD TIME IS THE CHARM

I'm not making this shit up!

There I am in the same area on I-80, I come around the same damn corner and there is another one of Iowa's fucking finest, and yes, he pulls out behind me as I pass by.

This time I don't even wait for the lights. I pull right over. He parks behind me and <u>then</u> turns his lights on.

He comes to the passenger side and is holding a weird looking gauge in his hand. Like the others, he looks like a kid. Is this some weird initiation ritual for rookies? Do they put these kids out here and tell them to check for dark windows as a way to get them out of the office?

"Good morning. The reason I stopped you is your windows are too dark."

"I know. I've been pulled over before. In this very same area, actually."

Now for whatever reason, this time I hadn't opened the passenger window all the way. It's probably seventy-five percent down. He takes this weird gauge he's holding and places it on the part of the window that's still up.

"Yep. See. It's too dark."

"My car is registered in Oregon. These windows are legal in Oregon."

"I'm going to need to see your drivers license and registration, please."

I hand him my driver's license, my registration, my insurance card, and the two other warnings I've been given the previous two years. I don't throw things out.

"What are these?"

"These are the last two warnings I've been given in Iowa the last two years about my windows being too dark. And if you'll notice, they've all been given to me in this area within a few days of the same date each year!"

He doesn't even look at them, he just hands them back.

"I don't need these."

I put them back in the glove box, knowing they'll soon be joined by another warning.

"I figured you knew something was up when you pulled over so quickly. Would you mind getting out of the car, sir?"

I will give it to these Iowa guys, they are polite.

Once again I'm sitting in the passenger side of his car while he's checking out my license and registration and asking me the same damn questions.

And yes, he gives me a third written warning about my windows. And again I bring up the fact that I've received these before.

"Yes, I see that you have been warned before."

"And since I don't live in Iowa and neither does my van, how can I prevent this every time I drive through."

"I'm not sure what to tell you. As long as these windows are illegal in Iowa you can be pulled over. Here is your warning.

Have a nice day."

"Yeah, you too."

The following year I find a route that goes from Nebraska though Kansas to Illinois on an old two-lane highway totally bypassing Iowa. It takes an extra hour, but it's worth it.

One year because of flooding, my detour takes an extra three hours and it's still worth it!

What is it about tinted windows?

ONE MORE TIME

So I'm doing a spring tour and I have a couple bookings in Northern Iowa and I think, "Fuck it!" I'll just deal with this. And it all goes well until…

I'm still in Iowa, heading toward Chicago, when suddenly this asshole in a VW comes flying past me doing at least ninety.

Sure, there are never any cops around when someone's actually breaking the law. This guy's just lucky his windows aren't tinted.

Something catches my eye and I check my side mirror. Way back in the distance I see flashing lights.

Okay, there is such a thing as karma.

I'm cruising along, doing the speed limit, when I realize that the state trooper should have passed by now. I glance over to my side view mirror and I don't see him. That's because he's right next to the van and staring at me!

Are you fucking kidding me?

I look at him like, "What the fuck?" I am incredulous.

He should be chasing a speeder who's obviously breaking the law and he's slowing down to check me out.

"Sure, pull me over and give me another warning for my tinted windows instead of going after someone who's actually breaking the law!"

Maybe he can hear my thoughts, I don't know.

Suddenly he gives me this weak wave and takes off after the VW. I keep driving hoping that I see him with the VW pulled over. I never do.

WTF, Iowa?

WE ALL HAVE RITUALS...

When I'm returning home I have a ritual that, up until now, only Fiona knew about. About a hundred miles from home I put on Social Distortion's *Somewhere Between Heaven And Hell*, and crank it up. And I mean *crank it up!* Most of the time I feel like I'm somewhere between those two places although I can honestly say I've spent time in both. This CD signals the end of a tour.

I love the road but it's a grind. I love being at home with my kid and when I'm home too long I feel the moss starting to grow on me. It's the joys of being a road dog.

I text Fiona, "Social D is in."

Her reply is always, "What time are you picking me up?"

I go straight to her school, or to her mother's house, and get her before I go home. That's the heaven part of my trip.

It always takes a good five or six days to decompress. Very few people know I'm home for the first week. I don't want to see anyone that I don't need to see, because I have to re-acclimate.

I've read about bands having difficulty adjusting to "normal life" for the first few weeks after a massive tour. I thought it was all bullshit. It's not. When your days are spent traveling, working, being in a different place almost every day, and constantly meeting new people, it wears on you.

There are a few things I need when I get off the road.

I need food in the house so I can make whatever I want to eat. I usually stop by the store to pick up a few things before I go home because I'm sick and tired of eating out and/or eating whatever is in the damn cooler.

I stop at my local grocery store and run in and out as quickly as I can. So, naturally, I run into people I haven't seen in years and of course they want to "catch up." I try to be friendly, or at least not a dick, but the last thing I want to do is engage in any conversation besides the one I'm having with my kid. I make some sort of half-assed excuse and apologize to them as I walk away. "I don't mean to be a dick, I just can't engage with you right now."

I want to climb into my own bed and I want to be surrounded by familiar things. I don't care how many hotels, motels, guest rooms or couches you sleep on, there is something about your own space that enables you to ultimately relax.

And Social Distortion makes that re-entry into home life a little easier.

ALL THINGS MUST PASS

Moses is a rescue. He was eighteen months old when I got him. The first time my vet checked him out she told me he was very healthy but because of his size, he would probably only live to be ten. I refuse to believe that.

It's why I don't feed him human food and I make sure we walk every day. I want him to be in good shape. I need him in good shape. He's my traveling companion.

He was seven when we started touring, and after five years on the road, he's slowing down. For the last couple years he's had trouble with his back legs. It's harder for him to jump in and out of the van but the biggest problem is stairs.

When we stay with Joe in Kansas City, there's a small flight of stairs at the back of the house that we come and go through. Moses walks up to the bottom of the stairs and stops. I come up behind him, lean over and put my right arm underneath his hips. In one motion I lift his hips, and his back legs, a few inches off the ground. As soon as Moses feels his legs lift up he starts walking up the stairs on his front paws with me lifting his rear legs like a wheelbarrow. As soon as we get to the top, I place his legs back on the ground and he walks in the back door.

A lot of friends ask when I'm going to stop taking him on tour since it's harder for him to get around. Moses will let me know when he's ready.

Moses is a road dog and it doesn't matter how old he gets. He wants to be with me wherever I am. The most important thing is for the two of us to be together. I can't imagine leaving him at home while I take off for months.

Over and over again I've been told that dogs need a routine. They want to be walked at certain times, fed at certain times and any change in the routine upsets them. I think that's more a reflection of the owners than the dogs.

When you get locked into a routine, I believe you live just a little less. Having your life revolve around certain things done at certain times might be fine for you, but not for me. I can't tell you how many times I'm asked how can I tour so much? People always tell me how much they hate not sleeping in their own bed at night.

That's unfortunate.

When I'm on tour, every day is an adventure and I love that part of it. Yes, I'm sleeping in different beds almost every night but I'm also meeting new people and experiencing new things.

I believe Moses is wired the same way, and if he isn't wired that way then he certainly adapted quickly. The only routine he and I have is that there is no routine.

As Moses ages there are some things I don't notice, or choose to ignore.

In Nashville we're walking with friends at this very nice park. It's just a three-or-four-mile walk, something Mo and I do all the time. The weather is warm, not hot, but there is high humidity. What I don't realize is how hard the humidity is on him. Moses is panting furiously. He stops and lies down. He doesn't want to get back up. I realize I haven't brought enough water with me. None of us have.

One of the members of our group volunteers to go get her car from the parking lot and take him back to the van where his bed and water bowl is. We wait as she goes and gets her car and I help him into it. She tells us to continue and she'll meet us back at the parking lot. When we get back she and Moses are laying in the shade, he has a full water bowl and is quite happy.

I feel bad afterward, thinking it should have been me that had taken him back to the van. I should have brought his travel bowl and more water with us on the walk. I don't realize how much he's aging, or I don't want to. It's a weird feeling to play this back in my head.

You get used to something or somebody and when they start changing you don't notice it right away. As the tour progresses

I'm much more conscious of his condition and make sure we never go anywhere without water.

This tour is no different than any other. We're seeing old friends and making new ones. Moses is slower and certainly sleeping more than he has in the past, but he's still game for anything. He's enjoying himself wherever we go and seems really happy. He still loves our walks and leaving his mark all of the country.

As he's gotten older I've become less strict about his diet. I give him some cheese or treats from whatever it is that I'm having. It's never a lot but I can see that big old tail wagging as he wolfs it down.

It doesn't seem like there's anything wrong with him, besides old age. We pull into Tulsa to stay with friends. They're not home yet so Moses and I sit on their front porch and wait. I take a photo of him lying at my feet. He's very serene.

The next day it's on to Fort Worth where I'm doing a couple of workshops at a film festival. Mark, the organizer is aware that I'm bringing Moses and I'm told we're booked in a hotel that's dog-friendly.

From the road I ask him to confirm that. He calls back and says it's no problem as long as the dog is under twenty pounds.

"In that case tell the hotel I'm bringing six dogs."

There's a moment of silence.

"He's that big?"

"Yeah, but he's old and very mellow."

"Let me get back to you."

He calls back shortly.

"If it's alright with you, you guys can stay with me. I have a fenced backyard, and two dogs that get along with everyone."

Moses spends the evening in the backyard playing with Mark's two dogs. Everything's good.

I decide to sleep on the couch in the living room, as the stairs to the second floor are too steep for Moses to climb. I get his bed from the van and lay it on the floor next to me.

In the middle of the night Moses wakes me up. He's sick. He throws up everywhere. That isn't like him. I figure maybe it's the heat.

I clean the floor, get Moses back on to his bed, and he goes right to sleep.

The next morning, he's still asleep. I take a shower and have breakfast. I take him outside so he can do his business. It's obvious he's not feeling well and he's having some trouble walking. He doesn't sniff or relieve himself at all. I bring him back inside and help him to his bed. He collapses on it and goes back to sleep.

We have a long day at the festival and Mark says it's okay to leave Moses at the house as his other dogs are there and it's cooler in the house.

We return about eight in the evening. I'm putting my workshop stuff back in the van when Mark comes out and says I'd better come in.

I walk into the living room and there's Moses lying on his bed all stretched out exactly like I left him. He passed away some time during the day.

All I can hope is that he died in his sleep having a running dream.

It's really rough seeing this. So many feelings run through me. The first one is guilt. I feel awful that he died alone, that I wasn't there.

I'm also in shock. There is nothing that has prepared me for this moment. I sit down beside him and pet him. I know he's gone but I still want to pet him.

I'm thinking about a lot of things. His tail wagging whenever he'd get out of the van to explore. Seeing him swimming and being so happy to be in the water. I see him pushing himself between my legs so I can pet him while talking to other people, and almost knocking me over. Lying at my feet in the sunshine at an outdoor patio while I have lunch. Pushing me off the bed as he stretches out on a too-small motel bed. And putting his head in my lap when I'm writing because he wants to be petted. I remember watching him sleep and he always looked so small and peaceful all curled up. I could still see the puppy that was inside. How I wished I could have had him as a puppy, I'm sure he was cute as hell.

Shit, now what am I going to do?

I suddenly feel really bad because Moses has died in the living room of a guy I hardly know. And I wasn't there.

Mark's amazing. He checks the Internet and finds a place we

can take Moses that night. It just doesn't seem like a good idea to leave him there in the living room overnight.

We carry him to the van and drive about forty minutes to an all-night emergency animal hospital. The people there are great and I make arrangements to have Moses cremated and the ashes sent to me in Portland. I'm not ready to let him go.

We drive back in silence.

When we get back to the house, we have some major cleaning to do in the living room. I'm still numb and Mark tells me to grab a beer, go outside and sit on the porch, he'll take care of it. He's a hell of a guy.

It's a strange feeling to be staying with someone you don't know and have your dog pass away in his living room. I feel awkward, embarrassed, sad, and all sorts of other things. Luckily, Mark is a dog guy and I'm not sure if he's taking it all in stride, but he's certainly fooling me if he isn't.

I can't imagine what would have happened if I'd been staying by myself at a hotel.

If we would've stayed at the hotel would Moses have passed away? If so, what would I have done? Did he eat something in Mark's backyard that sickened him? Or was it the night before in Tulsa? Was he poisoned? All sorts of irrational thoughts slam against each other in my head.

Mark comes outside with a beer and sits down. He says I don't have to go back to the festival the next day. He can cancel my workshop and explain to people what happened.

I go back to the festival the next day and do my workshop. I can't just stay at the house. I can still see where Moses had been laying when I came in. I can still feel his presence. I have to do something.

I wait until the evening to call Fiona and tell her. I'd like to say that I held my emotions in check, but I didn't. It was a hard phone call to make. We talked for a while and honestly she, at seventeen, was the more mature one on the phone. She calls me later to make sure I'm okay. I can hear the worry in her voice. I tell her I'm fine. I'm lying.

The next morning I get up, post a notice on the Internet about Moses passing and hit the road.

I'm deluged with wonderful comments from so many people. Some email and some call to make sure I'm okay. I lie to them and say yes. They tell me how much they loved Moses.

I head east, not sure where to go. I have a few days before my next gig and all I know is that I need to get out of Fort Worth and drive. Driving always makes me feel better. I can drive for hours in silence and the world stays away. Everything is okay when I'm moving.

My phone rings. It's Joe in Kansas City. He saw the post and feels awful. He loved Moses too. Where am I headed? I didn't know, I'm just driving. Joe tells me to come to Kansas City and stay with him. I don't have to do anything, just hang out.

Joe's words are exactly what I need. I arrive in Kansas City that evening. Others call as well telling me to come stay with them. The outpouring is amazing.

As I drive I keep looking to the back of the van to check on Moses. There's nothing there. I stop for gas or at a rest stop and instinctively go to the other side of the van to let him out. It's not until I open the sliding door that I realize he's not there.

I stay with Joe for three days. We go out and eat, listen to music, and I walk. I walk all over Joe's neighborhood, where Moses and I used to go. I need to get out and move. I also need to sit quietly and process. Staying with Joe allows me to do both.

I have difficulty sleeping. I'm used to sharing the futon with a giant dog that tries to take all the blankets. It feels good to stay at Joe's, but I have other gigs and a tour to finish.

I'm asked if I should just cancel the rest of the tour and go home. I can't do that. Moses and I started this tour together and I really feel the need to finish what we started. I'm also dreading going home because when I get there it'll really sink in that he isn't with me.

Everywhere I go on the rest of the tour people are wonderful. The Moses tributes keep pouring in. It makes me feel good that he was so well loved by so many people.

After three weeks, it's time to head home. I'm still looking in the back of the van expecting to see him. I may be crazy but there are times when I feel him back there. He's still with me.

I call Fiona and pick her up as soon as I hit Portland. We go home and hang out. The reality of Moses being gone is hitting me hard.

I think back to what my Vet said so long ago. That Moses might live to be ten years old because of his size.

Moses passed away a week before his twelfth birthday. We beat the estimate of his life span by almost two years, and we had a blast doing it.

I miss you, buddy.

POSTSCRIPT

I do a couple more tours after Moses' death and they're good, but they're not the same. People ask me why I don't just get another dog?

I can't. I'm not ready.

I recall the words of my buddy Eric, "You know, if a man is lucky he will have two great dogs in his life. I've had three and I feel truly blessed."

I know I'm really blessed, because I've had four.

I've had some great dogs, but Moses was special. He was my companion, he was a family member, and he was always there and ready for the next adventure even when he got old. You don't replace that.

Moses taught me a lot about patience, loyalty, tolerance, and to always turn around three times before lying down. (I stole that last part from Robert Benchley.) He didn't care where he was or what we were doing as long as he was with me. He was always up for meeting new people and knew when to curl up next to me when I was troubled. He would lie down in the back of a classroom or auditorium and stay there until I told him it was okay to get up and stretch his legs. He never complained about traffic or if we were running late. Moses lived in the moment and didn't worry about things out of his control.

Since he's been gone I've worked hard to be more like him. Only time will tell if I succeed.

Four years after Moses passed, another "rescue" came into my life, Mickey. He's a mere ninety pounds but an equally enthusiastic chocolate Lab. We have yet to do any touring, but I'm sure that's just a matter of time.

I look forward to taking him to a lot of Moses' old stomping grounds. Who knows, maybe as Mickey is sniffing around someplace he'll get a whiff of Moses' scent. God knows he marked in enough places.

I feel his presence every day and there are some nights when I'm absolutely convinced that he's still hogging the bed.

MOSES
(1997 – 2009)
Always in my heart.

GLOSSARY

Kicking Bird – My third feature film is the story of Martin "Bird" Johnson, a 17-year-old "white trash" high school kid who runs. With his mother in jail, his father gone, one brother in a juvenile work camp, and his bitter grandfather beating him, there is nothing else to do but run! One day the manipulative high school cross country coach sees Martin outrun his entire team, (they want to beat him up), and thinks that Martin is his ticket to a college coaching position. This feature length film was made for around $5,000. (Yeah I wouldn't believe that either but I was there and we really did it.)

The Garden of Eden – Not the Bible one, the one in Kansas. If you want to know about the Bible one you can read that book. Better yet go to http://www.garden-of-eden-lucas-kansas.com/ and read about this one. And if you're ever in Lucas, Kansas, you should check it out. S.P. Dinsmoor (see below) used over 113 tons of concrete to make his Garden of Eden and I'm not sure how much of that he used to encase his wife after she died. It's kinda creepy but worth a stop.

S.P. Dinsmoor – A Civil War veteran who came back home, joined the Masons, and started thinking about things differently after witnessing all of the slaughter during the war. He was called a free thinker and apparently Ohio was considered a hotbed of free-thought activity. Go figure. Eventually he moved to Kansas and designed his Garden of Eden as one part home and one part income producer. To learn more about him check out the Garden of Eden website and Wikipedia - https://en.wikipedia.org/wiki/Samuel_P._Dinsmoor.

Ray Bradbury – A prolific author who has influenced so many people. He had the ability to write with the enthusiasm of a thirteen-year-old boy.

Which is pretty amazing. My favorite books by him are *Something Wicked This Way Comes*, *Fahrenheit 451*, and *The Illustrated Man*. But you know what? Read anything by him and you can't go wrong. If you haven't read anything by him, you're an idiot. If you don't want to be an idiot then go pick up a book. Enough said.

Boeing – You know these guys, they make jets.

John Steinbeck – The author of *Travels With Charley*, *The Grapes of Wrath*, *Of Mice and Men*, *Cannery Row*, *East of Eden*, and thirty more books, give or take. If you've gone to high school in the last forty years, odds are you've had to read at least one book by Steinbeck, but don't hold that against him. One of my all time favorite writers.

Jack Kerouac – Author of *On The Road*, *The Dharma Bums*, *The Subterraneans*, among others. These books are usually read by first-year college students and English majors. Most young writers want to imagine themselves as one of the Beat writers without the alcohol problems.

***Zen and the Art of Motorcycle Maintenance*, by Robert M. Pirsig** – One of the books everyone read in the seventies when they were stoned and talked about how amazing it was. If you re-read it when you're not stoned you'll find it boring, pretentious, ponderous, and almost as unreadable as anything by Tom Robbins, another author best read when you're young and stoned.

Two-Lane Blacktop – A low-budget road movie directed by Monte Hellman featuring James Taylor, Dennis Wilson, Warren Oates and an iconic '55 Chevy. It's called a cult classic but it bombed when it was released back in 1971. Almost all car guys love that Chevy and I actually think that Dennis Wilson is great in the film because he rarely ever says anything. The man knew his strengths as an actor. Check it out.

Easy Rider – A 1969 road film that was supposedly written by Peter Fonda, Dennis Hopper, and Terry Southern but if you can find a story anywhere in this film please let me know. And what was up with that drug trip scene in New Orleans? Was that too long and boring or what? I remember this film most because my older sister snuck me in to our local movie theater to see it when I was thirteen. I left upset, outraged, and angry at the ending like most viewers under thirty did. I saw it years later when I was in film school and cringed at the sixties language and vibe. It may be a classic but it doesn't age well.

Don Quixote – A novel by Miguel de Cervantes originally published in 1615. This novel is most notable for the scene in which Don Quixote imagines that windmills are monsters and he charges them on his faithful horse Rocinante. Needless to say he loses. Terry Gilliam has been trying to turn this novel into a film for years. Check out *Lost in La Mancha*, an amazing film about his efforts. I also have a phrase from the book tattooed on my arm. And, no, you can't see it.

My Short Films - I've made eight short films that have been seen all over the world including PBS and Canadian and Australian television. They've been shown at film festivals including London, Sydney, Annecy, Sao Paulo, Sundance, Chicago, Aspen, Mill Valley and Edinburgh. Titles include: *That Really Obscure Object of Desire*, *You'll Change*, *Stolen Toyota*, *Friday Night*, *Enough With the Salmon*, *Love the One You're With*, *Tales From I-5*, and *I Think I Was An Alcoholic*, (with John Callahan). You can buy them from me or I'm sure they're lurking around YouTube someplace.

Birddog – My first feature tells the story of Harv Beckman, a used car salesman in a trashy part of town who accidentally comes in to possession of a rare 1948 Kaiser automobile, which leads to some disturbing revelations about the facts behind the 1948 Vanport, Oregon, flood which destroyed an entire city. Portland, Oregon, is the backdrop of this film that explores racism, greed, and class in a very corrupt city. Throw in the local Kiwanis Club and you have a very odd unpredictable film.

The Gas Café – Five people collide in a bar one night. One is dead. One never lived. And the other three are lying. My second feature was shot in digital video in 8 nights. It was funded entirely on unemployment checks.

Gus Van Sant – A filmmaker whom I worked with on six of his films. From *My Own Private Idaho* to *Finding Forrester*. It was an interesting time…

Fiona – My kid.

The A Team – A really bad television show from the eighties that features a bunch of ex-special forces soldiers who don't swear. They shoot automatic weapons and blow shit up but no one is ever killed or even really hurt. It's a bad live action cartoon, I suppose, and responsible for giving us Mr. T. Those bastards!

"Squeal like a pig!" – A notorious line from the John Boorman film *Deliverance*. If you don't know what this line means, then I'd suggest you watch the damn movie. You'll never forget it.

Pat's and Gino's – Cheese steak restaurants in Philadelphia that each have their fanatical followers. I don't mean to piss off any Philly folks but I still can't figure out why you can only eat at one. It seems kind of foolish.

SWAMP (Southwest Alternate Media Project) – A really cool non-profit media organization in Houston that has been dedicated to independent media since 1977. They host workshops, screenings, and conferences, and do everything they can to promote and support independent filmmakers. They have a show called *The Territory*, which is the longest running PBS showcase for independent film. Anyone who's anyone has had their work featured on this show. Including me. Check them out at http://swamp.org/.

Lloyd Kaufman – Troma Entertainment – If you haven't seen a Troma film then you've been living under a rock. Lloyd and his partner Michael Herz combined to bring us such classics as *The Toxic Avenger*, *Class of Nuke 'Em High*, and *Poultrygeist: Night of the Chicken Dead*. Lloyd has helped a lot of filmmakers get their start and remains a very accessible guy. But he needs to lose the saddle shoes…

SXSW – A great Austin, Texas, music festival that also shows films.

Walmart – A series of campgrounds with stores attached that stretch across the United States. The campgrounds are known for their low prices (free) and for the fact that they have multiplied like rabbits across the country. Just remember, don't drink the water or buy the food. But the restrooms are nice. Usually.

DC Shorts Film Festival – The premiere short film festival not just in the US but all over the world. They always program incredible films and take care of the filmmakers who come to the festival. If you have a film programmed here by all means go. It's really a festival for filmmakers.

The Monaco, Washington, D.C. – A part of Kimpton Hotels. Dog-friendly and kind of expensive unless someone else is paying for the room. The staff is amazing and the beds are really comfortable.

Motel 6 – Dog-friendly and much cheaper. For the most part the staff ignores you except when you're checking in and the rooms are livable.

AT&T – phone carrier I no longer use because of their lousy coverage.

MCI – Defunct long distance carrier that after many mergers and scandals was eventually purchased by Verizon. These guys are not missed.

Ohio – A state I drive through quite often but rarely stop in.

Touch of Evil – Orson Welles film starring Charlton Heston as a Mexican detective. No, I'm not buying that casting either but it is one of my all time favorite films. Orson Welles was a master.

USC – My overpriced alma mater. Although I do enjoy it when they get beat in football.

The *Star Wars* Films – An ATM that George Lucas used to own. Once he milked it to death he sold it to Disney, who are in the process of merchandising the hell out of it in order to make back the ridiculous amount of money they paid for it. Also a film series that started in the 1970s that has attracted a faithful legion of whiners and complainers who rarely like anything since the third installment *Return of the Jedi*, which came out in 1983. Damn, that's a long time to whine.

Green Day – A punk band from Northern California that, according to legend, has played in hundreds of kids' basements all over the U.S. for days at a time. It makes you wonder how they made any money on the road.

Idaho – A mythical place in the United States where nothing ever happens and I get blamed for it anyway.

Angry Filmmaker T-shirts – Apparently they're made in Nicaragua, purchased in the U.S., silk-screened in Portland, Oregon, and are still subject to import duties by American immigration authorities with small penises.

UFVA (University Film and Video Association) – An academic association made up of film, video and digital media professors and instructors.

Woody Allen – A filmmaker who used to make comedies where everyone sounds like him. Mostly works in Europe now.

PBS affiliates – a loose network of television stations that has no problem overpaying for films by people like Ken Burns and yet wants most other filmmakers to give them their work for free. Especially if you're local. They're best known for pledge drives that never stop and continuing to air *The Moody Blues at Red Rocks* from 1992.

Hank Williams – A country and western singer who wrote a lot of songs that will break your heart. Too many singers try to emulate him. He was an original. And his grave is a nice place to go in the evenings, have a beer, and think about life.

Southern Poverty Law Center – A dedicated group of people who put their lives on the line to make sure that people are treated decently. They strive for equal rights for all and are one of the nicest groups of people I've ever met. Please support their mission.

Nightingale Theater (Tulsa, OK) – One of my all time favorite places to play in the US. The folks who run this place do a lot of original and experimental work and they've been doing it for years. You gotta respect that! Check them out next time you're near Tulsa.

Glory Hole – A hole cut in a wall at about waist level usually found in some questionable bathroom stalls. Some people use them to slide their dicks through and hope that the person on the other side will help them achieve an orgasm.

Christ of the Ozarks – I'm sure people think this place is really cool but it creeps me out. I didn't stay for the *Passion Play* or whatever the performance was, but seeing this giant weird looking statue out in the middle of the woods is just bizarre. If you're anywhere near Eureka Springs, Arkansas, you have to check this out.

Siskiyous – A small mountain range bordering Southern Oregon and Northern California. Incredibly scenic during the spring, summer, and fall. A real pain in the ass in the winter.

Radar Love **by Golden Earring** – A song about a trucker's love for his mate and he dies in the end. A staple of classic rock radio, just don't listen to this song late at night on dark highways.

One Flew Over the Cuckoo's Nest – The novel by Ken Kesey. I read this book in elementary school and was blown away by the way Kesey paints a picture of the patients and staff at a mental hospital in Oregon. The novel is from the POV of "Chief" Bromden, which is why I've always felt that the Jack Nicholson film version pales in comparison, 'cause it's all about Jack. The novel is all about the Chief and it's amazing.

"Frankly, Scarlett, I don't give a damn!" – What I said to Scarlett Johansson when I broke up with her. Or a variation of an often misquoted line from the film *Gone With The Wind* (the actual line is "Frankly, my dear, I don't give a damn").

Studs Terkel – One of the great writers/storytellers of our time. His books are oral histories and his essays are great. Read this guy! You'll be entertained and you'll learn. What could be better?

Winchester Mystery House – A house built and added onto by a crazy lady. She was married to the guy who invented the Winchester repeating rifle. She believed she heard the voices of all of those who had been killed by the rifles and the only way to stop the voices was to continue to build on to the house. She slept in a different room every night so the spirits couldn't find her. Workers added on to this house twenty-four hours a day seven days a week for something like thirty-eight years! This place is a tribute to one of the craziest people in America. But she was incredibly wealthy so she was just considered eccentric.

Area 51 – The Visual Effects house in Los Angeles, not the place in New Mexico.

Terry Gilliam – One of the members of the great *Monty Python's Flying Circus* and a film director in his own right. The films he's made are among my favorites. Look him up on the Internet and start watching his films. You'll thank me later.

Oral Roberts University Prayer Tower – A two-hundred-foot tower in the middle of Oral Roberts University. It opened in 1967. It looks like something from the Jetsons and offers a three-hundred-sixty-degree view of the campus. It's not nearly as impressive as the Space Needle in Seattle, which is six-hundred-five-feet tall and has much better views.

Ernestine & Hazels' Bar & Grill – It's called the best dive bar in the country and I believe it. Of course it was a brothel at one point in its history. The building is old, dark and did I mention haunted? Oh yeah. Hit the low-key bar upstairs, listen to some music, and keep you eye out for past tenants and patrons who never left.

Tom Bodett – A spokesman for the Motel 6 chain (at least he was) who apparently is an author, voice actor, and radio host. He's the guy who says at the end of the commercials, "We'll leave the light on for you." He has never left a light on for me and I'm pretty sure he doesn't really stay at Motel 6 either.

Dada – An avant-garde art movement in the early 20th century. There's really a lot more to it than that and if I were you (and I once was) I'd look this up on my own.

Surrealism – A cultural movement in the early 1920s best known for visual artworks and writings. It developed out of the Dada movement and, trust me, it's much more accessible. Look at the work of the people listed below. That'll tell you much more about surrealism than I ever could.

Marcel Duchamp, Max Ernst, Salvador Dali, Hannah Hoch, Rene Magritte, and Paul Delvaux – Some of my favorite artists of all time. Do your homework and find out who they are. Then you can see how their work is still influencing people today.

Al fresco – A fancy way to say you're eating a meal outdoors but you don't wish to be mistaken for being homeless.

Rod Serling – An iconic screenwriter and television producer best known for his series *The Twilight Zone*, which fooled many people because he used a science fiction anthology series to deal with much broader issues. One of my favorite quotes of his is, *"In almost everything I've written, there is a thread of this: man's seemingly palpable need to dislike someone other than himself."* This guy was a genius!

Fulbright – The last name of the janitor at my elementary school who I'm sure had nothing to do with the (Fulbright) program for competitive merit-based grants for international studies. But I could be wrong.

Yuengling – A beer that comes from the U.S.'s oldest brewery, established in 1829. Best consumed in a small neighborhood bar in West Virginia with a couple of professional wrestlers.

Hooters – A restaurant that specializes in chicken wings and putting plastic bags full of ice in to your pitcher of beer. The food is pedestrian at best but they hire waitresses with large boobs hoping that you won't notice the mediocre food. Apparently it works.

AAA Guide Books – These books were incredibly useful on the road except for when they weren't. Most of the information is good but it tends to get outdated quickly. I'm happy all of their books exist, but I'm extremely happy that they continue to provide towing if you're a member. I'd never tour without these guys.

Jerry Garcia – A founding member of the Grateful Dead, a band whose fan base is practically a cult. I freely admit I went to see them in concert back in the early '70s when apparently they were at their peak. I got bored and left after the first hour. It was a decision I've never regretted. For some reason people think I look like him. (God I hope not, he's dead.) I did get to meet him one time in Berkeley (of course) and he was a very nice man.

Charles Manson – Another leader of a cult that people seem to think I bear a resemblance to. Mostly when I was younger and had dark hair. (I don't see this one at all.) Manson was responsible for the deaths of Sharon Tate and many others. He is still in prison and hopefully he stays there.

Franz Kafka – A writer most people know about but have never read. Take a few hours and read *The Trial*. The man was a genius and if you haven't read his work I probably think less of you.

Social Distortion – *Somewhere Between Heaven and Hell* – Sure, it came out in 1992, but it's still one of the all-time great records. A blend of country, rockabilly and punk. Trust me it works.

Made in the USA
Monee, IL
29 August 2019